Curious George™

Blast Off

UNIVERSAL©

05 06 07 08 EPG 10 9 8 7 6 5 4 3 2 1
14635 Curious George: Blast Off

Help the man with the yellow hat find George.

Start

Finish

You Can Draw!

Use the grid to draw George.

Dalmatian Press

How many words can you make from the letters in:

Grocery Shopping

ship

shore

Secret Message

Lift the bottom of the page toward you and
view from the bottom.

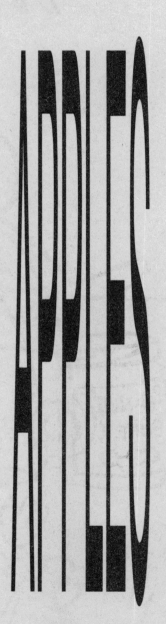

Answer: Apples

George makes a sandwich.

George is a curious little monkey.

Dalmatian Press

Let's play!

Dalmatian Press

Which picture is different?

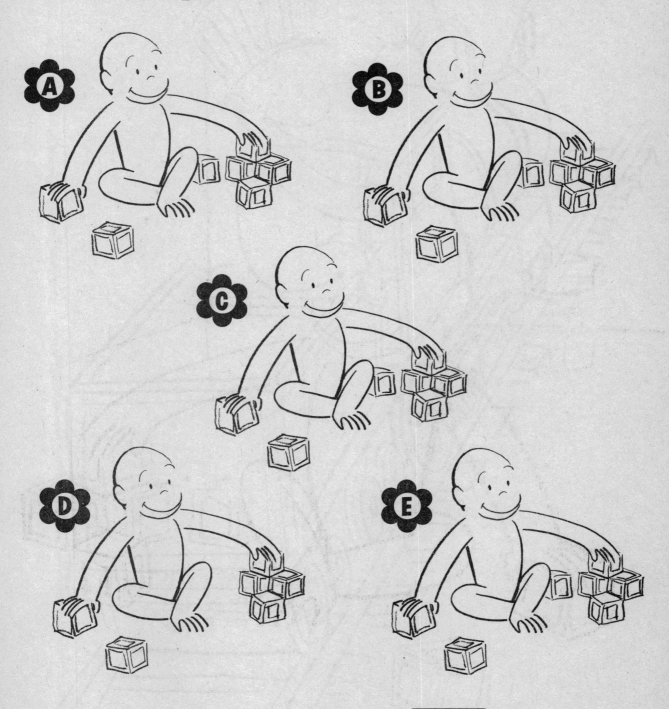

Your answer:

"Let's go see some animals,"
says the man with the yellow hat.

George is always curious about other animals.

RINGTOSS

There are fun games here!

Dalmatian Press

And peanuts for the animals!

Kangaroo

Look! Some friendly kangaroos!

George likes to share.

Which lion is different?

Your answer:

What a beautiful parrot!

Can you read, George?

Ostrich

Uh-oh!

Elephant

What a long nose!

Dalmatian Press

Elephants like peanuts.

Seal

A flippery friend.

Dalmatian Press

Seals like fish.

Which shadow matches the alligator?

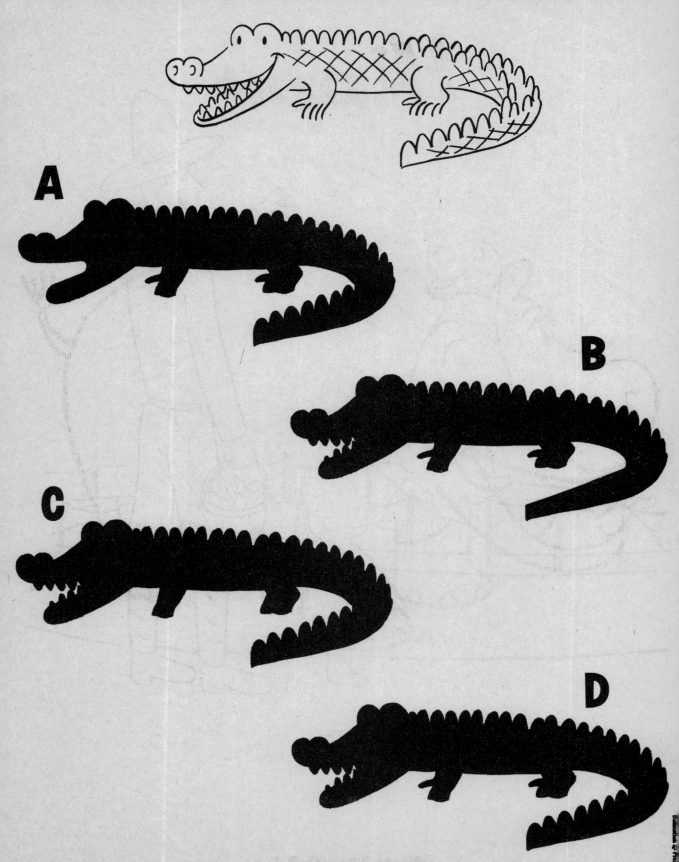

Hippo

What big teeth!

Koala

Koalas are good climbers—just like George.

Dalmatian Press

Lion

Look at that mane!

Rhino

What a sharp horn!

How many squirrels do you count?

Your answer:

Answer: 4

Giraffe

Look at that l-o-n-g neck!

Wheeeee!

George gives the bunny an extra-big hug.

Draw a line from each number to the matching number of animals.

1

2

3

4

5

Color By Number

1-gray   **2-brown**   **3-red**

Zooey Words!

Fill in the blanks to finish the puzzle.

Down

1. Seals like _____ .

2. Lions have a big _____ of fur.

Across

3. George feeds the animals _____ .

You Can Draw!

 Use the grid to draw the ostrich.

George loves bunnies!

Dalmatian Press

Circle the seal that leads to the ice cream.

6

Guess Who?

Circle your answer.

Chef

Giraffe

Rhino

Hippo

Finish the Picture

Be an artist!
Finish the picture of
Curious George on the
merry-go-round.

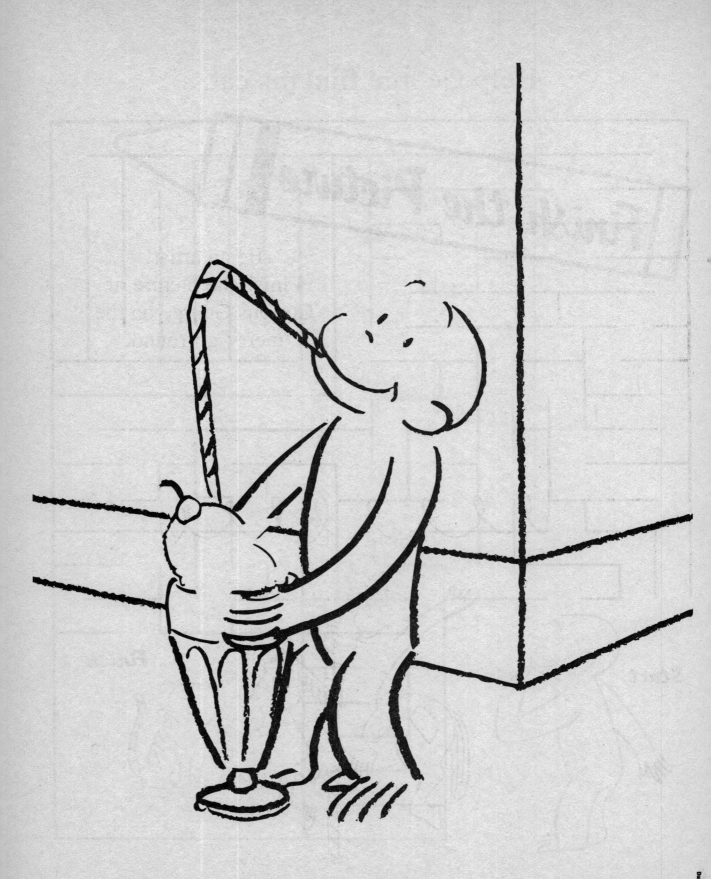

Help George find his cat.

Start

Finish

Dot to Dot

Connect the dots to finish the giraffe.

Dalmatian Press

No hands!

LIL'
BUCKAROO

Curious Words!

Fill in the blanks to finish the puzzle.

Down

1. Curious George is a curious little __monkey__.

2. George's best friend is the man with the yellow __hat__.

Across

3. George's favorite food is __bananas__.

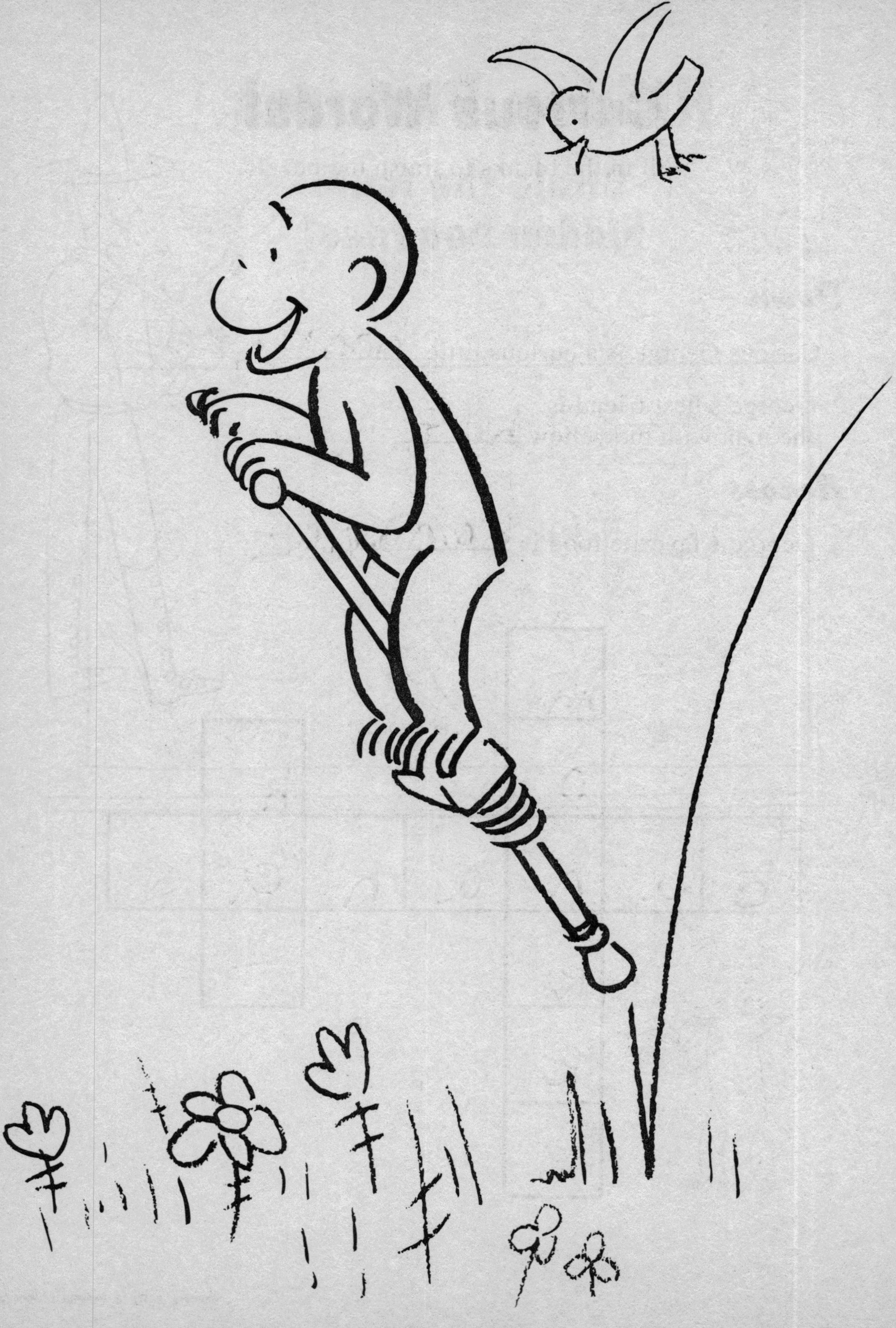

Hidden Pictures

Circle the four hidden bananas!

 — sign reading "THIS WAY TO THE MONKEYS"

Dot to Dot

Connect the dots to finish the picture.

Time for bed.

Aa Bb Cc Dd Ee Ff Gg

George knows the answer!

George likes books.

George writes a message.

You Can Draw!

Use the grid to draw
the man with the yellow hat.

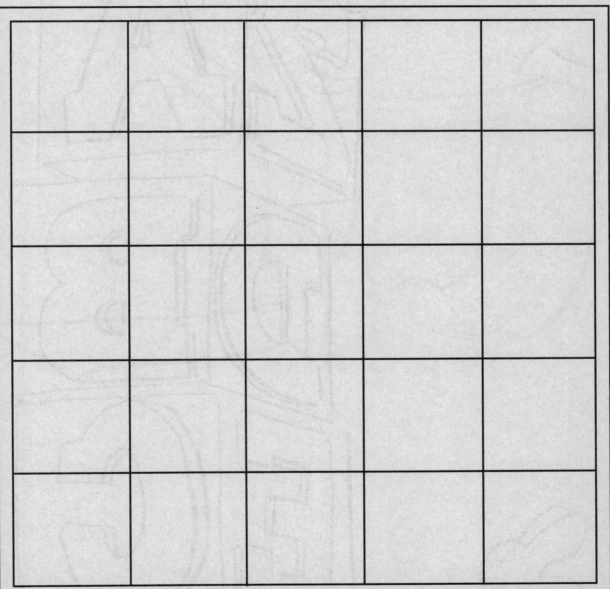

Finish the Picture

Be an artist!
Draw what George
is painting.

Help George paint a picture.

Monkeys love to swing!

Finish the Picture

Be an artist!
Draw the swing that
George is playing on.

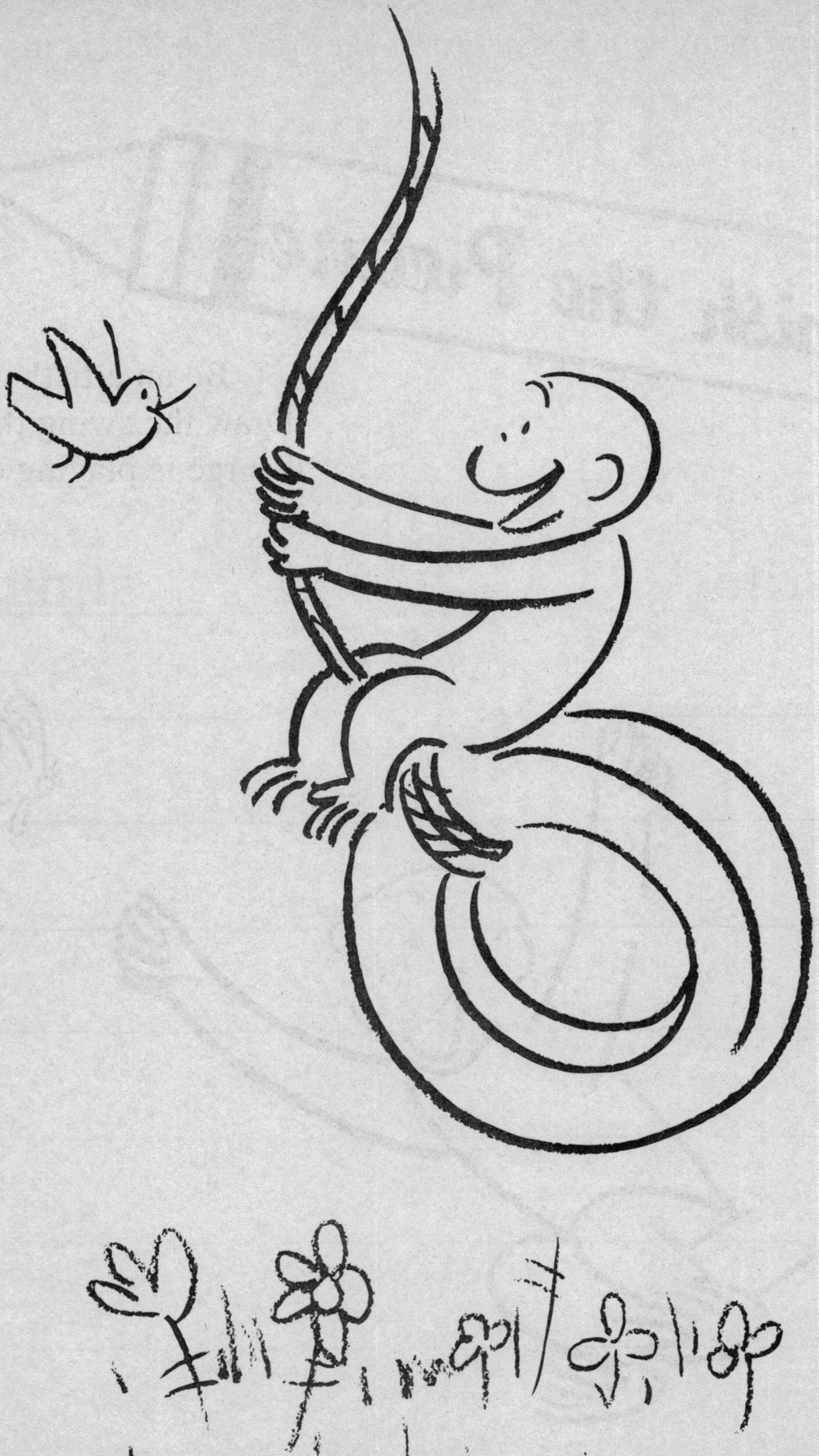

How many words can you make from the letters in:

Tire Swing

write

sting

Curious George makes a cake.

Extra-big lollipops!

Going Bananas

Color By Number

1-pink   **2-brown**   **3-red**

George likes spaghetti.

Connect the DOTS

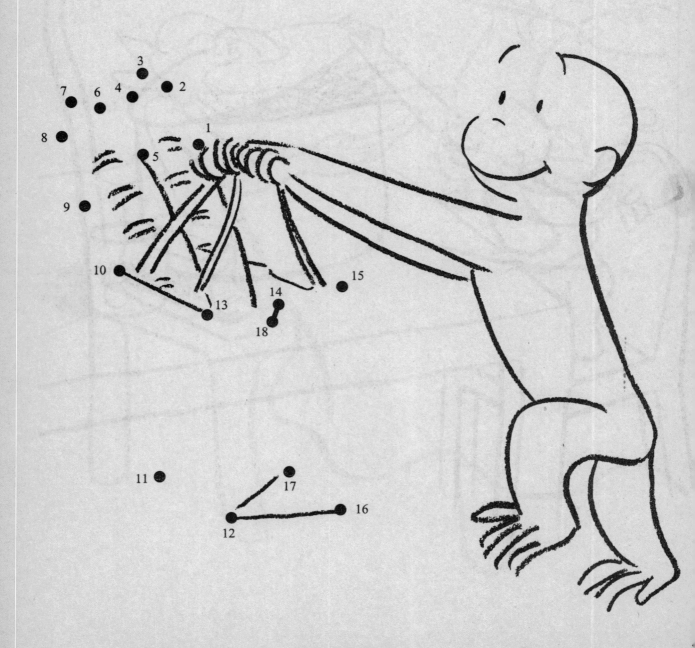

Books can even help George eat!

How many words can you make from the letters in:
Cookie Jar

are

_____

_____

_____

_____

_____

_____

joke

_____

_____

_____

_____

_____

_____

George likes pizza.

Secret Message

Lift the bottom of the page toward you and
view from the bottom.

Dalmatian Press

Piles and piles of spaghetti.

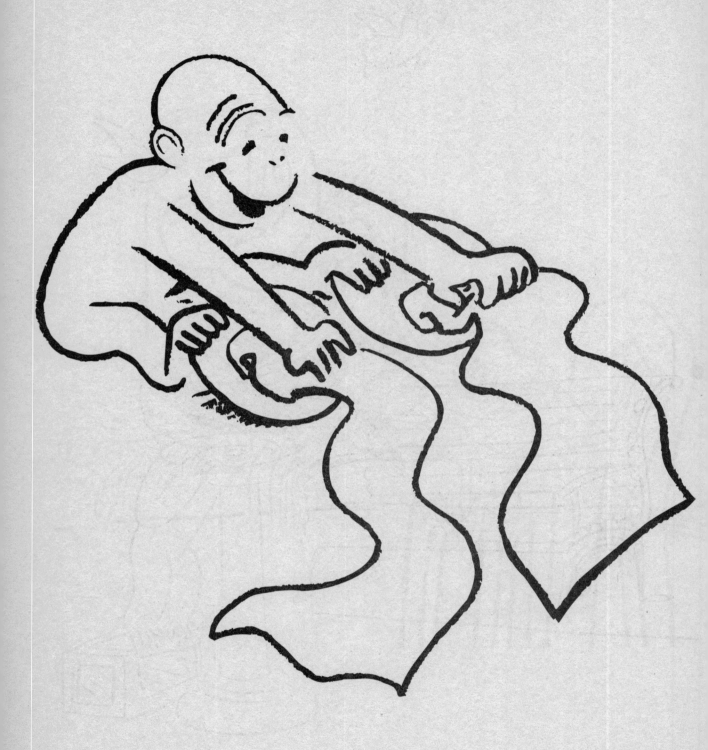

George helps out.

Dalmatian Press

Which picture is different?

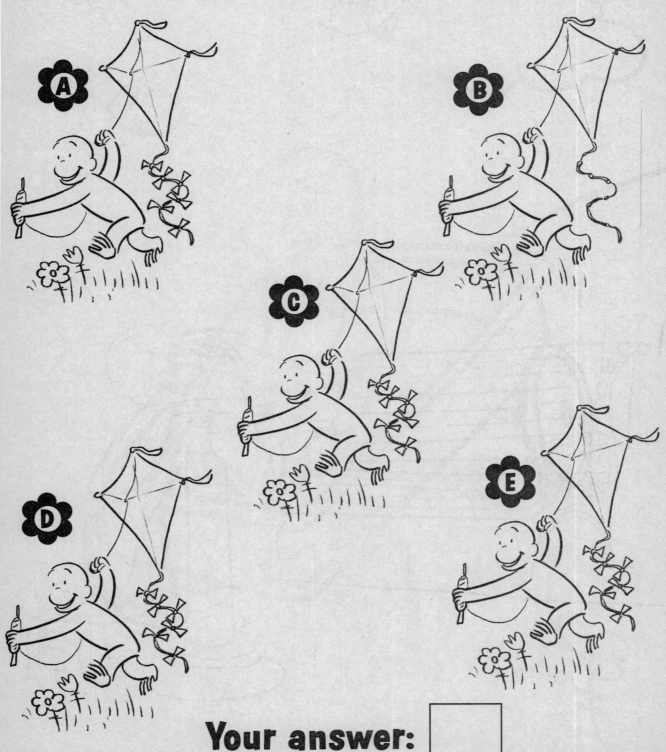

Your answer:

Down the hill.

George likes to read to the bunnies.

Which chocolate leads to the rhino?

Zoooom!

Dalmatian Press

Connect *the* DOTS

Astronaut George

Which picture is different?

Your answer:

You Can Draw!

Use the grid to draw
George smiling.

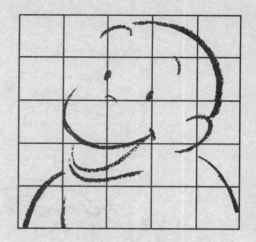

Dalmatian Press

Finish the Picture

Be an artist!
Draw the hose
Curious George
is playing with.

Fireman George

Secret Message

Lift the bottom of the page toward you and
view from the bottom.

Dalmatian Press

Which picture is different?

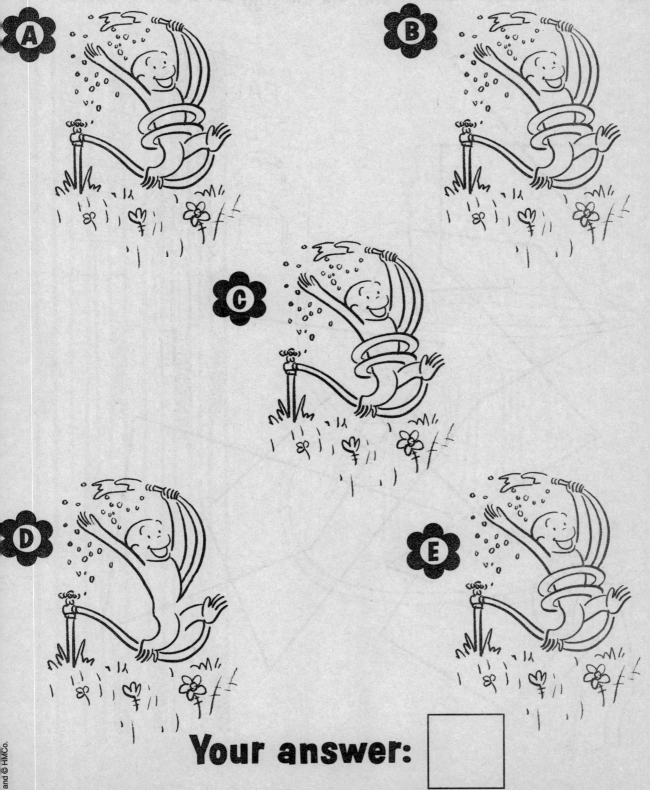

Your answer:

Which line leads George to the man with the yellow hat?

A

B

C

Which picture is different?

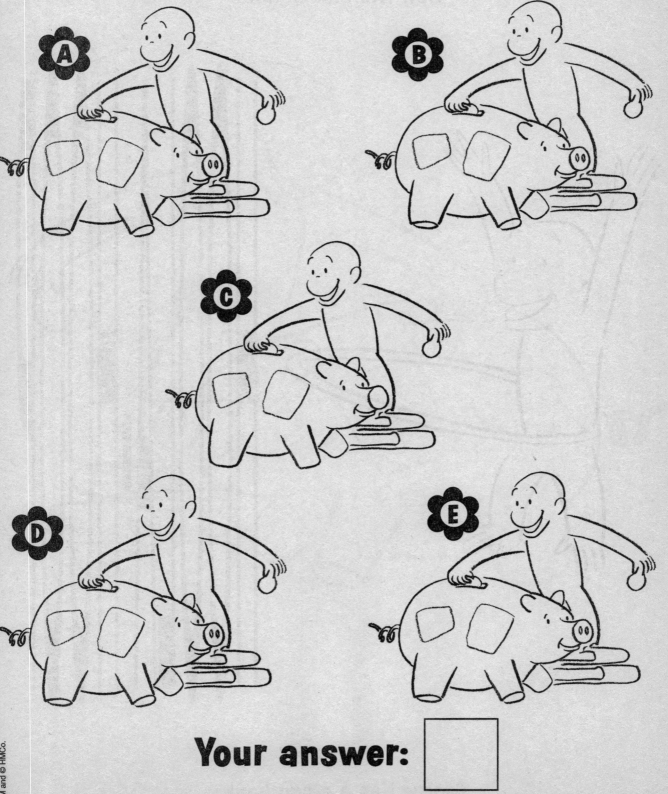

Your answer:

Secret Message

Lift the bottom of the page toward you and
view from the bottom.

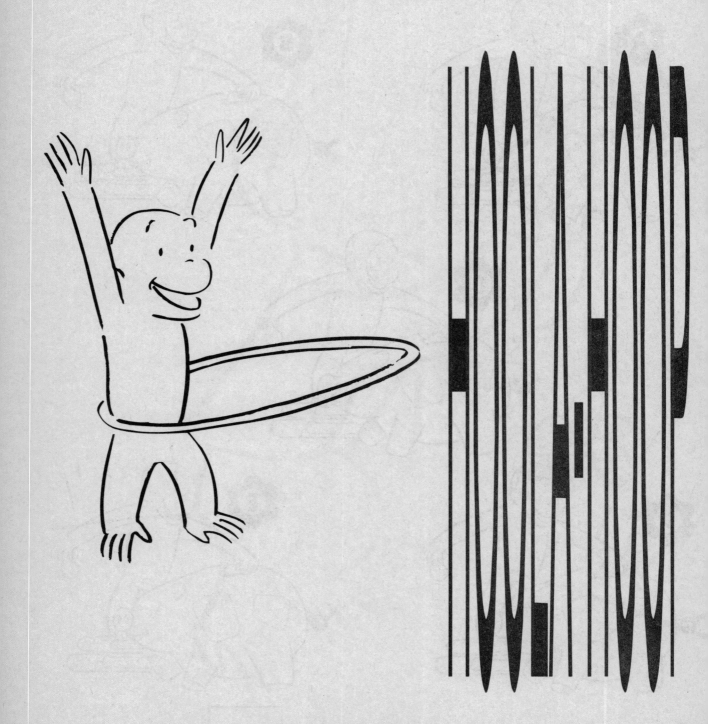

Dalmatian Press

150

Where shall we go next?

Draw a line from each item to its shadow.

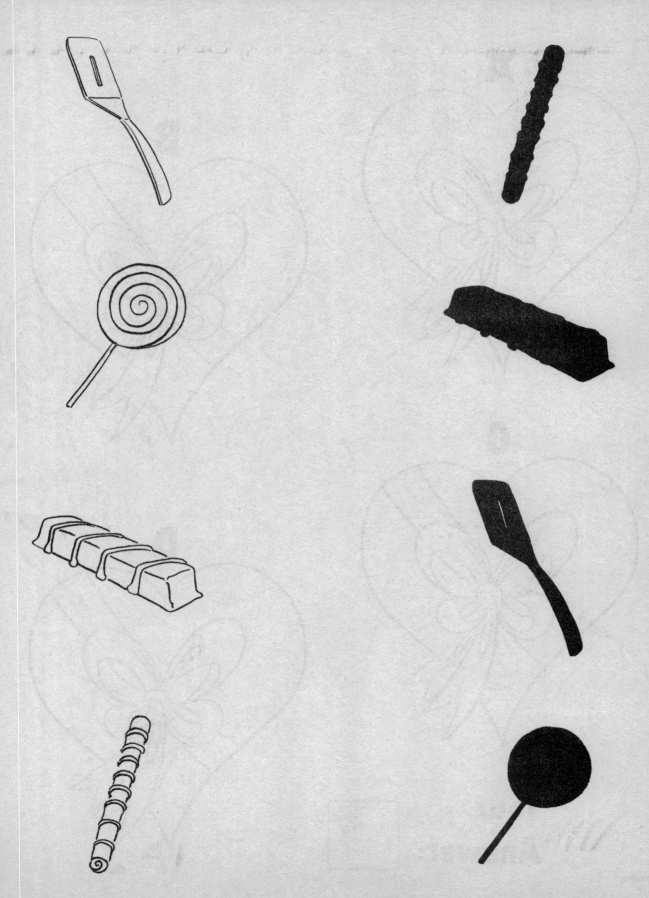

TM and © HMCo.

Which heart is different?

A

B

C

D

Your
Answer:

Dalmatian Press

Decorate the candy box.

Be good, George!

How many gumdrops
do you count?

Your answer:

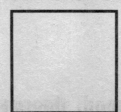

What could these be?

An extra-big lollipop!

George likes to share.

"Thank you, George."

You Can Draw!

Use the grid to draw Bunny.

Guess Who?

Circle your answer.

✿✿✿✿✿✿✿✿✿✿✿✿✿✿✿✿✿

Squirrel

Chef

Curious George

The man with the yellow hat

Find the squirrels who get the donuts.

1 2 3

A B C D E

173

Which picture is different?

A

B

C

D

Your answer:

It's a Party!

No, no, George! No fingers in the cake!

Which one is different?

A

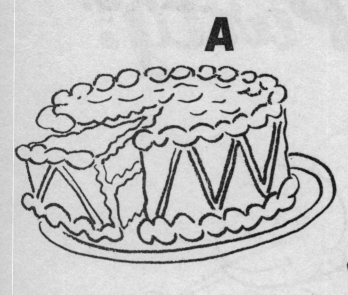

B

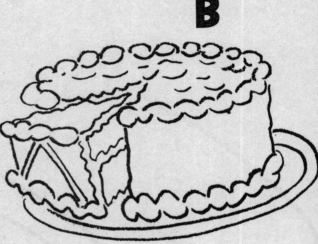

C

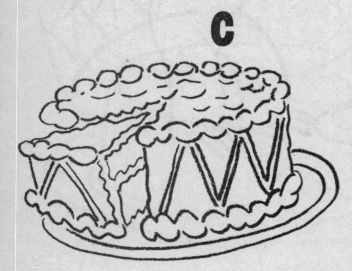

D

Your Answer:

Decorate the cake.

Now, George, you may have a slice!

George can help!

Dot to Dot

Connect the dots to finish the box.

Secret Message

Lift the bottom of the page toward you and view from the bottom.

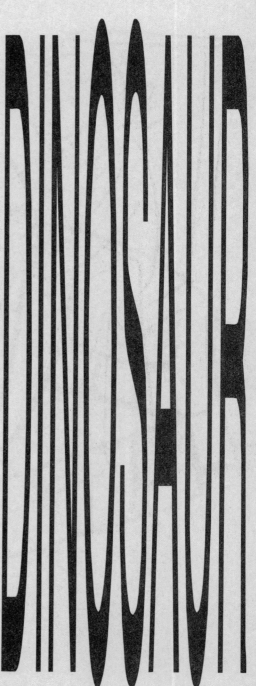

Hidden Pictures

Circle the four hidden ice-cream cones!

Circle which picture does not belong.

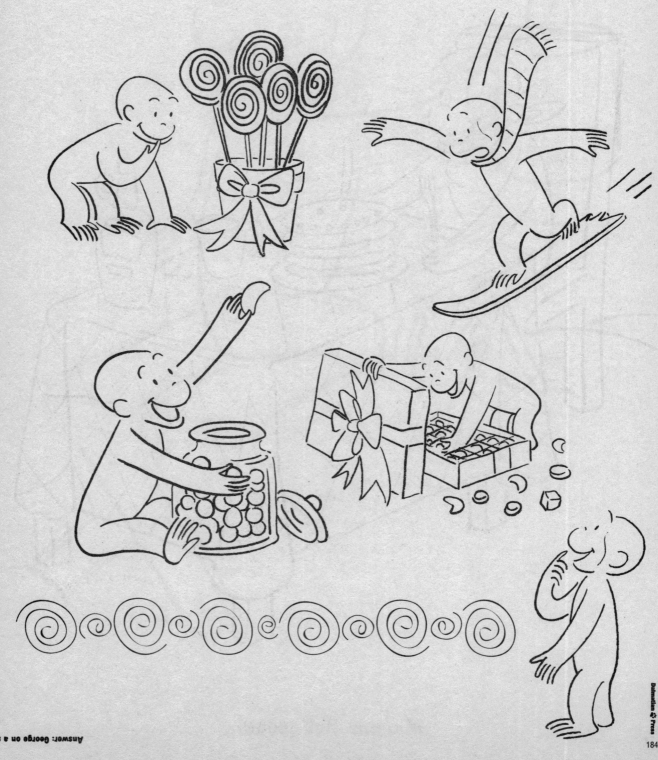

Mmmm. Hot cocoa!

You Can Draw!

Use the grid to draw
George and his bear.

Finish the Picture

Be an artist!
Draw the stars that
Curious George sees.

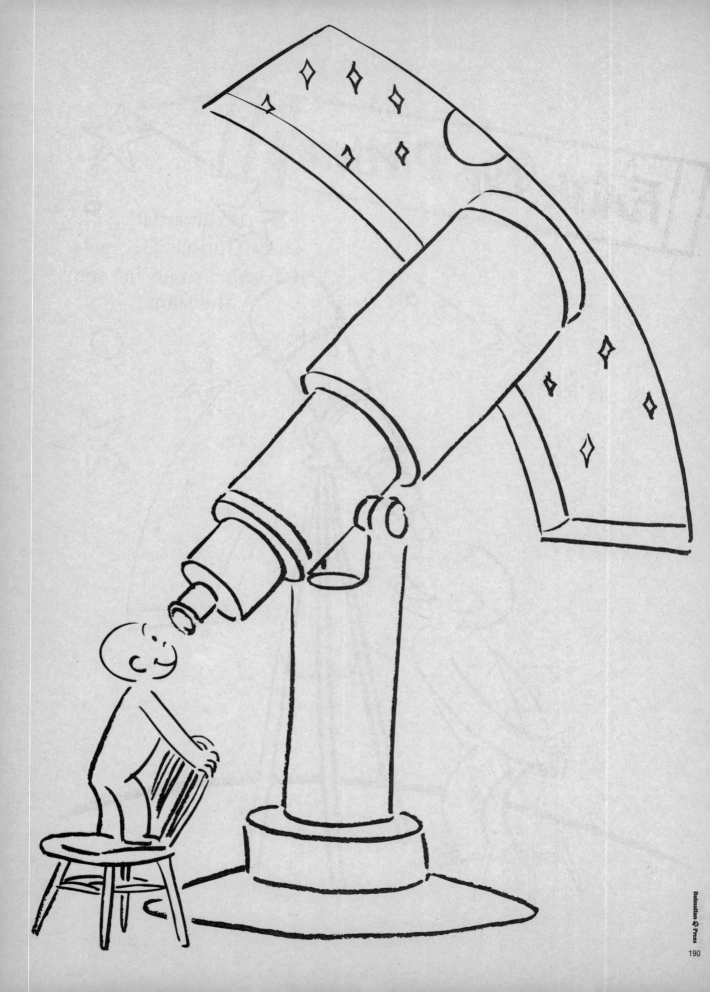

Finish the Picture

Be an artist!
Draw Curious George's
telescope so he can see
the stars.

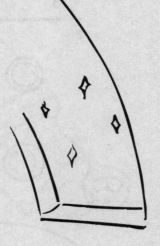

Dot to Dot

Connect the dots to finish the picture.

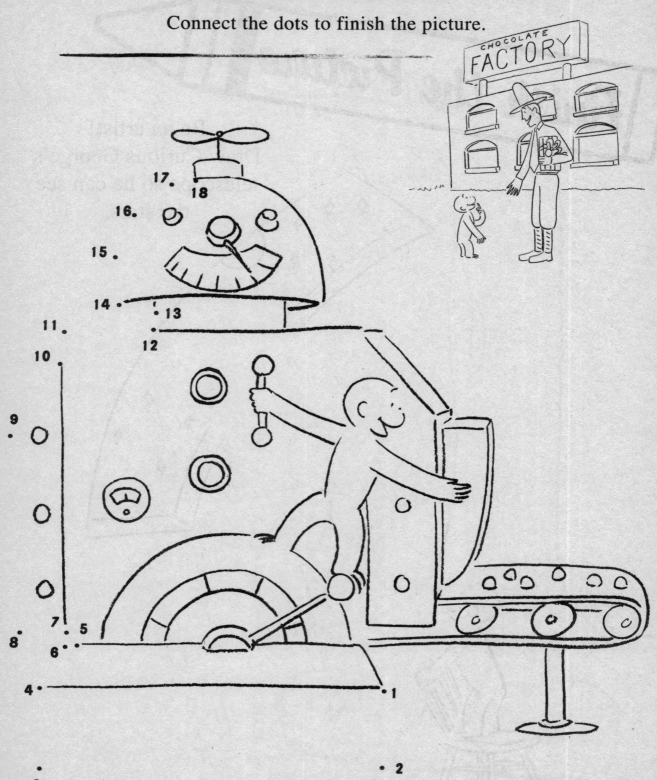

Bubbles for the birds!

Bubble fun!

Connect the DOTS

Help Curious George finish building the bird house.

How many birds do you count?

Your Answer: ☐

Playing pirate!

You Can Draw!

Use the grid to draw
George in his pirate hat.

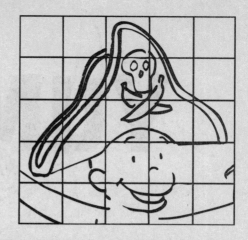

YUM YUM

Help George find the bunny.

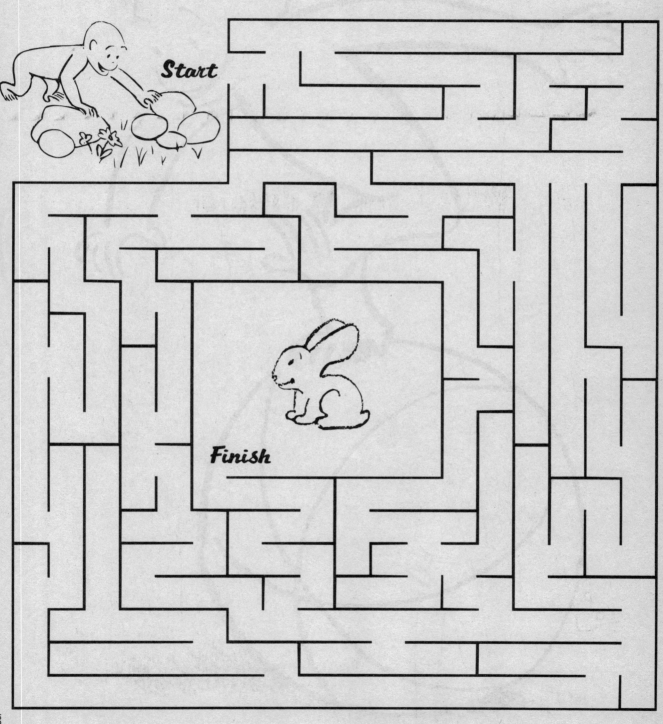

Start

Finish

George likes red apples.

How many words can you make from the letters in:

Candlestick

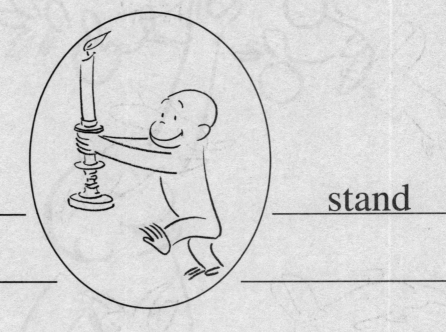

let

stand

How many bunnies are hopping around?

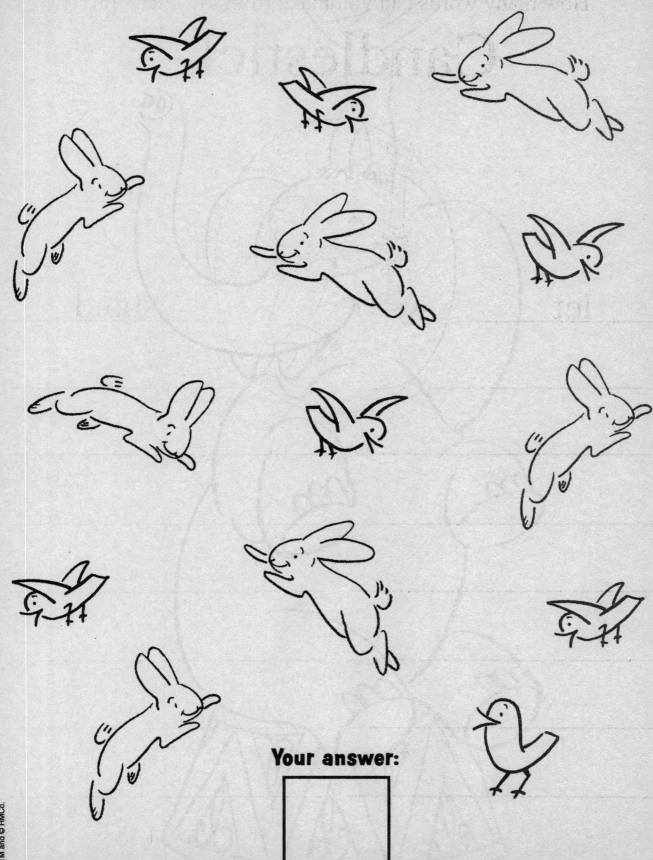

Your answer:

Answer: 7

Riding the waves.

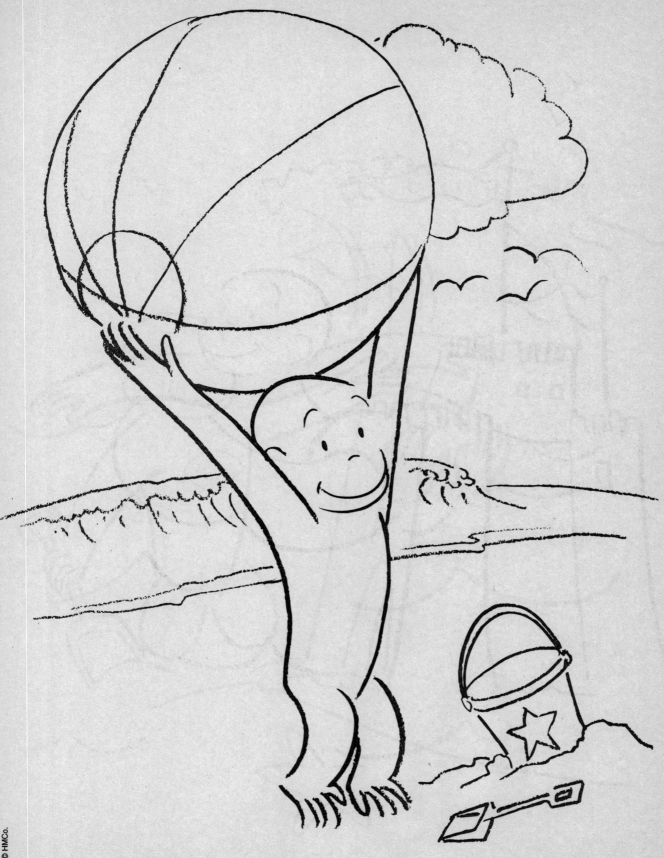

How many words can you make from the letters in:

Sand Castle

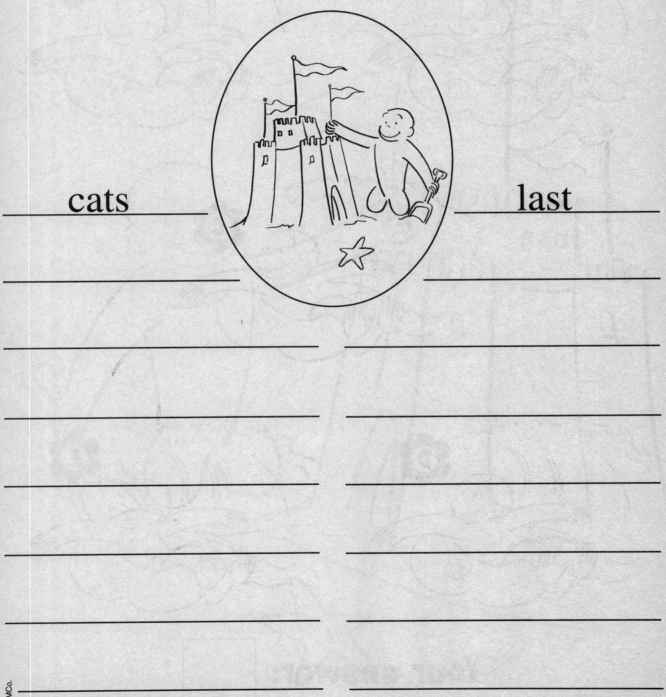

cats

last

Which picture is different?

Your answer:

Dalmatian Press

Help George find the sailboats.

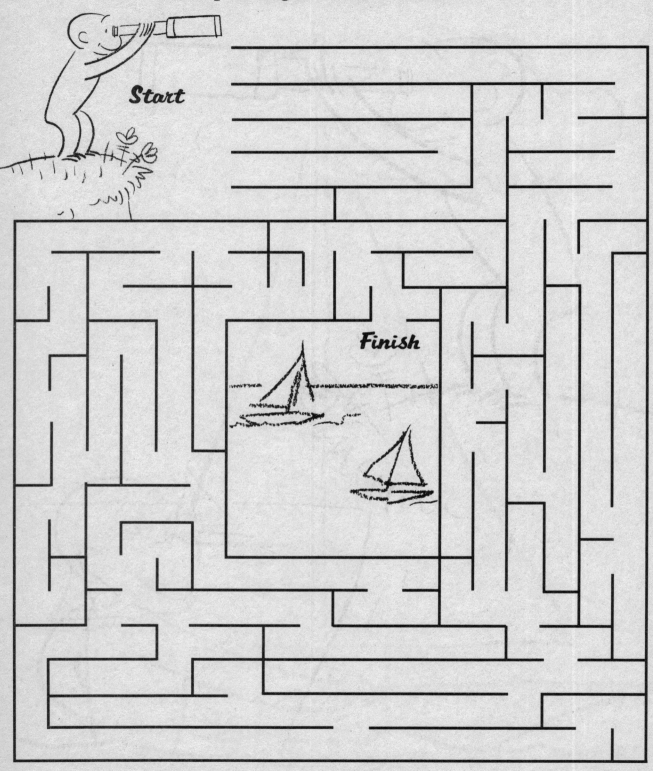

Start

Finish

Secret Message

Lift the bottom of the page toward you and
view from the bottom.

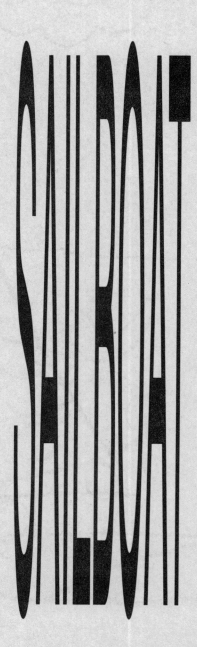

Dalmatian Press

How many words can you make from the letters in:

Diving Board

road

ring

An extra-big hug for the bunny.

235

Connect the DOTS

Dalmatian Press

Wheeeeee!

The man with the yellow hat took George to the ski slope.

Wheee! What fun George is having!

Help George find his way downhill.

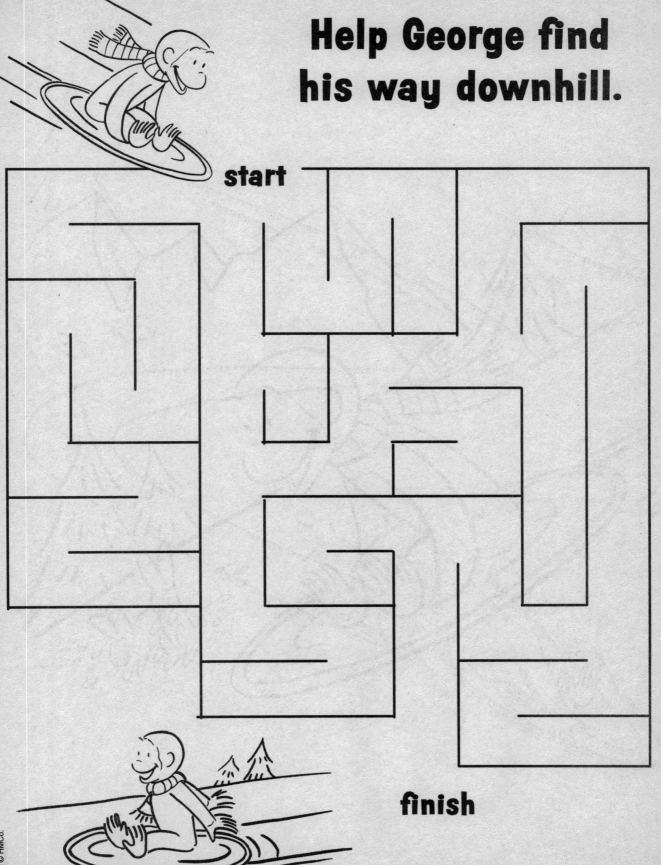

start

finish

Hello, bunnies!

Goodbye, bunnies!

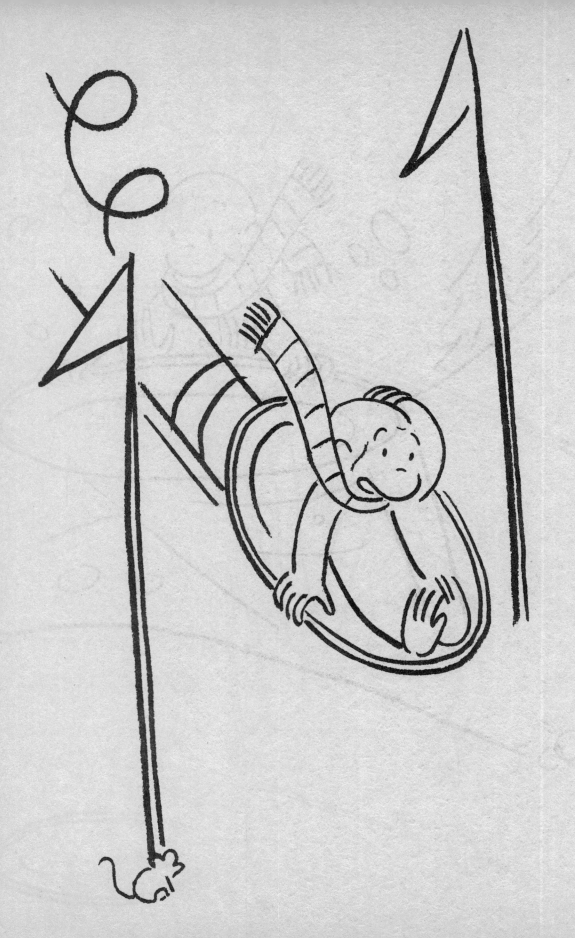

George is good at doing tricks...

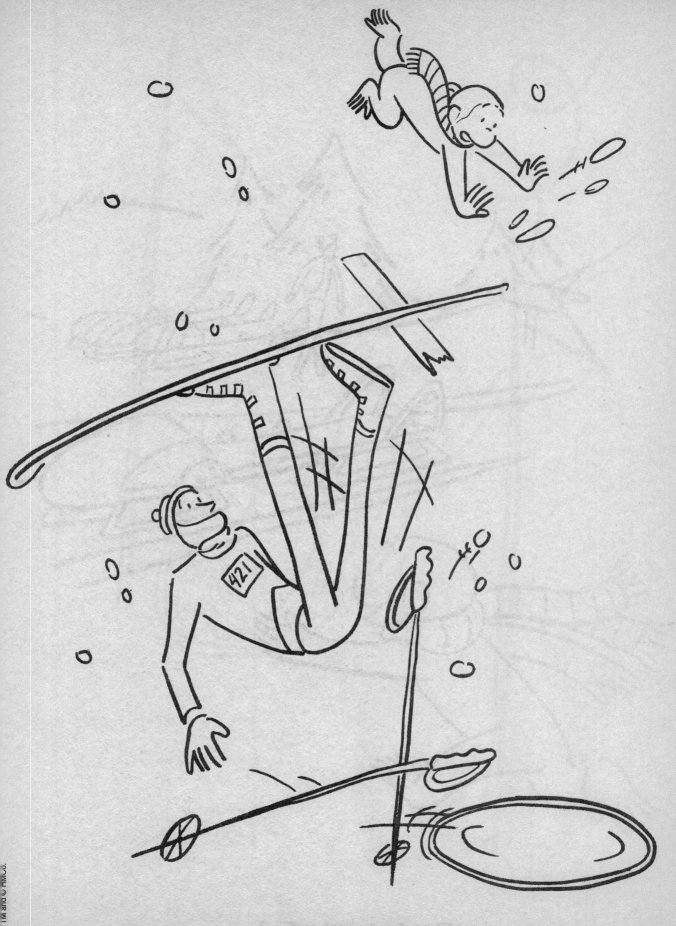

...and getting into trouble!

This looks like fun!

How does it go?

Oh! Like this!

Help George slide downhill.

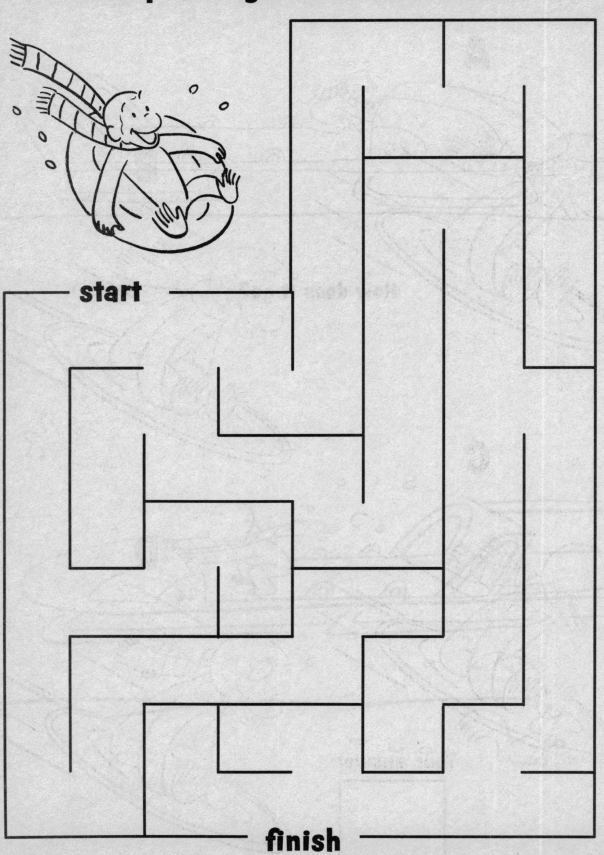

start

finish

Which one is different?

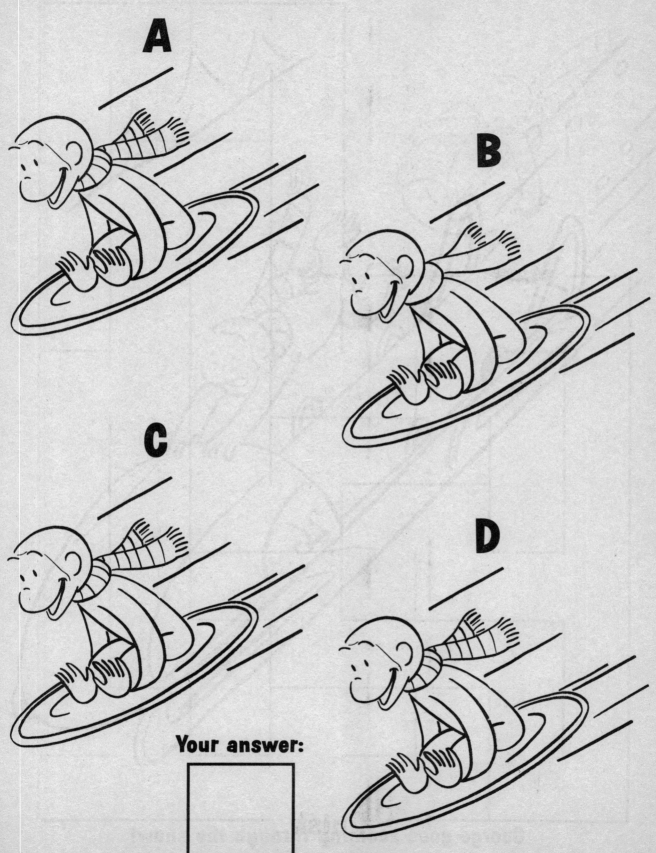

Your answer:

George goes zooming through the snow!

Dalmatian ♥ Press

Hidden Pictures
Circle the four hidden chocolates!

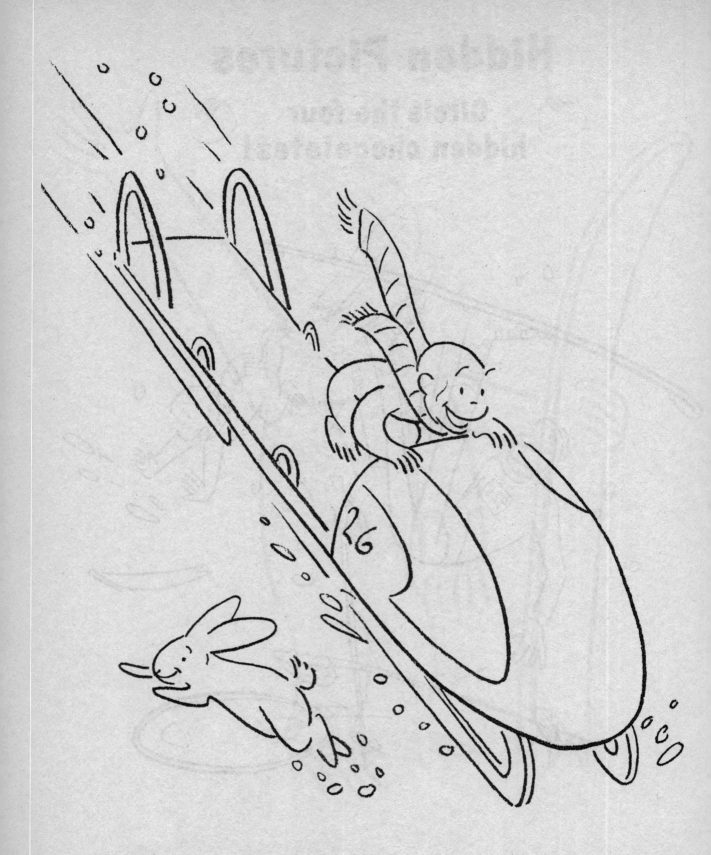

Everyone, out of the way!

George finds a snowboard.

Be careful, George!

The man with the yellow hat helps George!

Which one is different?

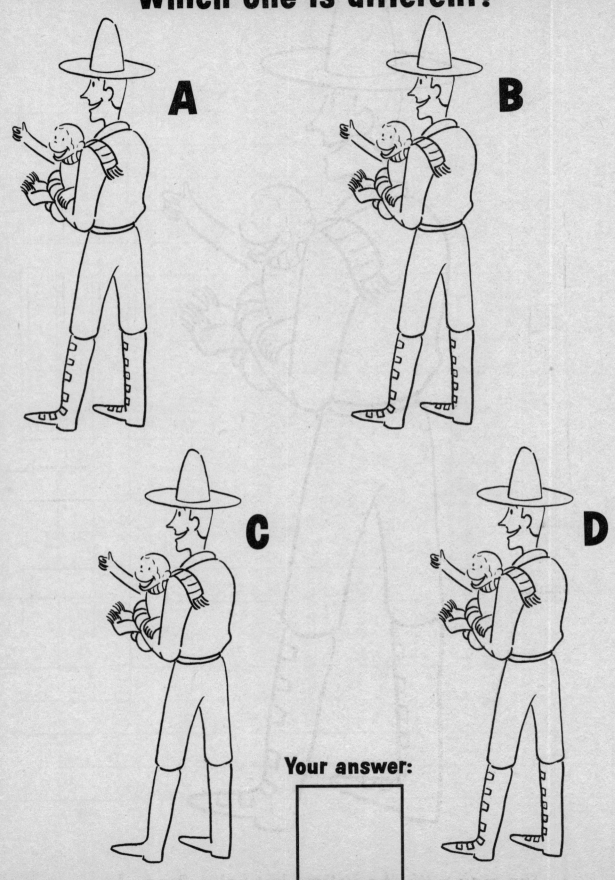

A

B

C

D

Your answer:

What a good little (curious) monkey.

Curious Crosswords!

Fill in the blanks to finish the puzzle.

Down

1. George likes to play in the _____.

Across

1. George likes to go _____ down snowy hills.

2. When it's cold outside, George likes to drink _____ cocoa.

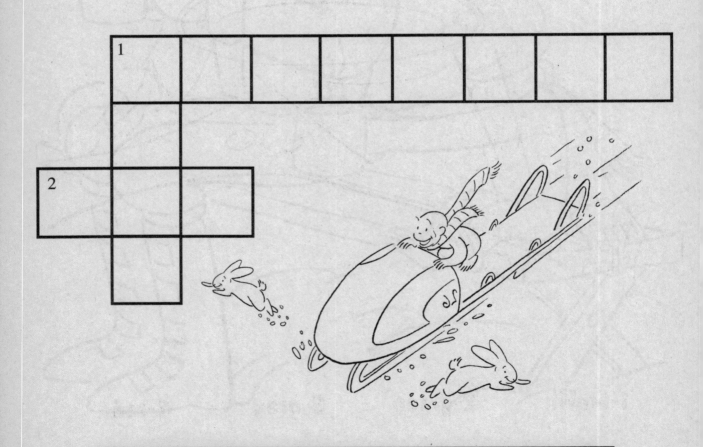

Dalmatian Press

Color By Number

1-brown   **2-green**   **3-gray**   **4-red**

Guess Who?

Circle your answer.

The man with the yellow hat

Giraffe

Lion

Chef

How many seals do you count?

Your answer:

261

You Can Draw!

Use the grid to draw George sledding.

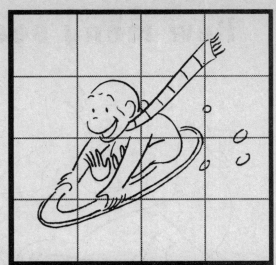

Dalmatian Press

Secret Message

Lift the bottom of the page toward you and
view from the bottom.

Answer: Hot Chocolate

Circle which picture does not belong.

267

Help George finish the snowman.

Start

Finish

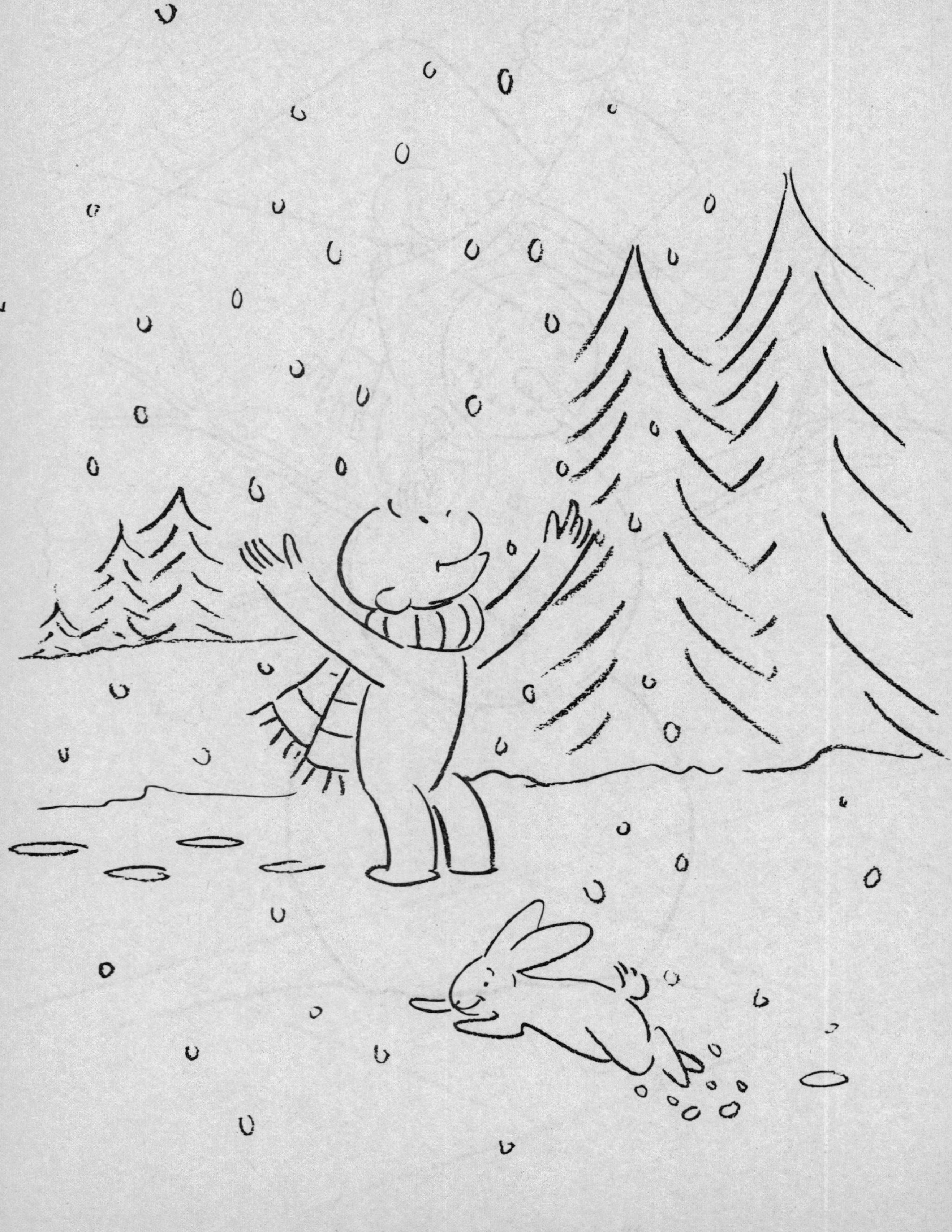

Making a snow angel.

Help George find the yellow hat.

Start

Finish

Mailing letters to friends.

Connect the DOTS

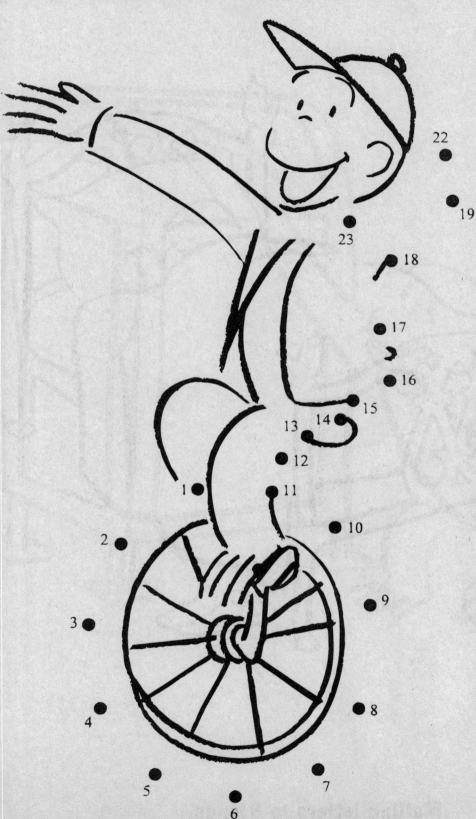

275

You Can Draw!

Use the grid to draw engineer George.

How many words can you make from the letters in:

Marching Band

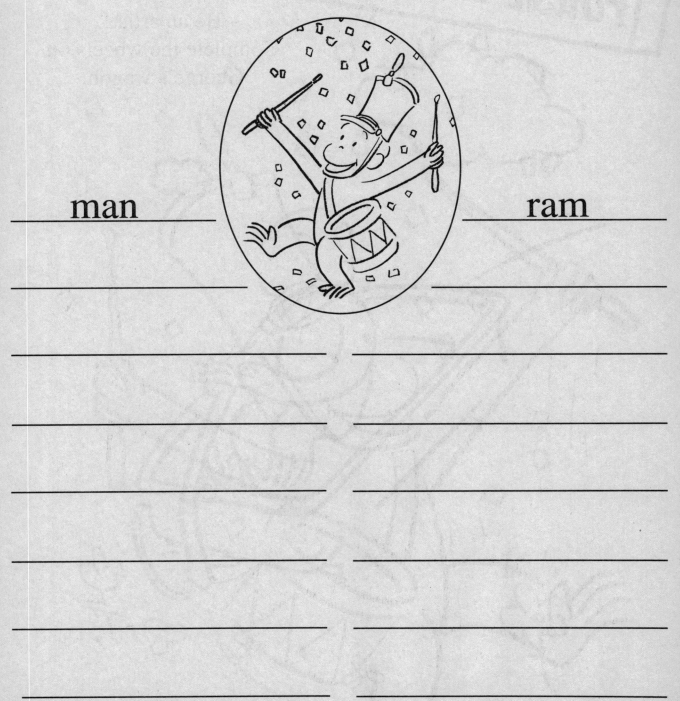

man

ram

Finish the Picture

Be an artist!
Complete the wheels on George's wagon.

281

Color By Number

🟤 1-brown
🟡 2-yellow
🔴 3-red

Dalmatian Press

George feeds the bunnies.

Finish the Picture

Be an artist!
Draw Curious George's
fish.

Match each to its shadow.

Write the correct letter in the box next to each shadow.

285

Help George catch the fish.

Start

Finish

Help George find the fish.

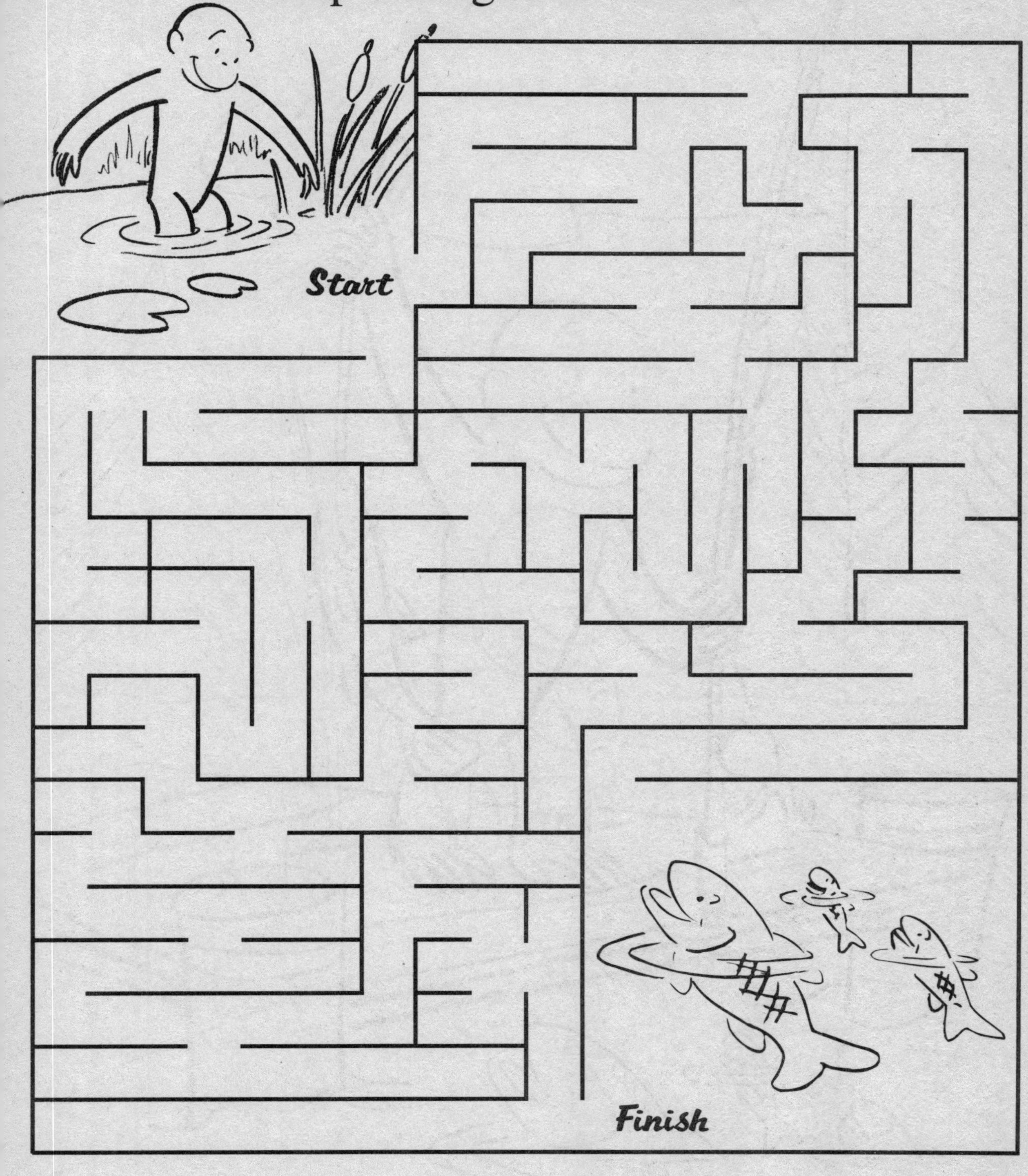

Start

Finish

Playing leapfrog

Playing leapfrog.

Help George find the lost frog.

Start

Finish

Secret Message

Lift the bottom of the page toward you and view from the bottom.

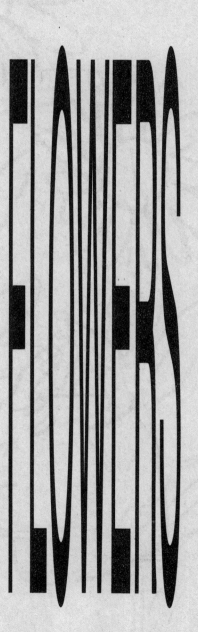

How many words can you make from the letters in:

Flower Garden

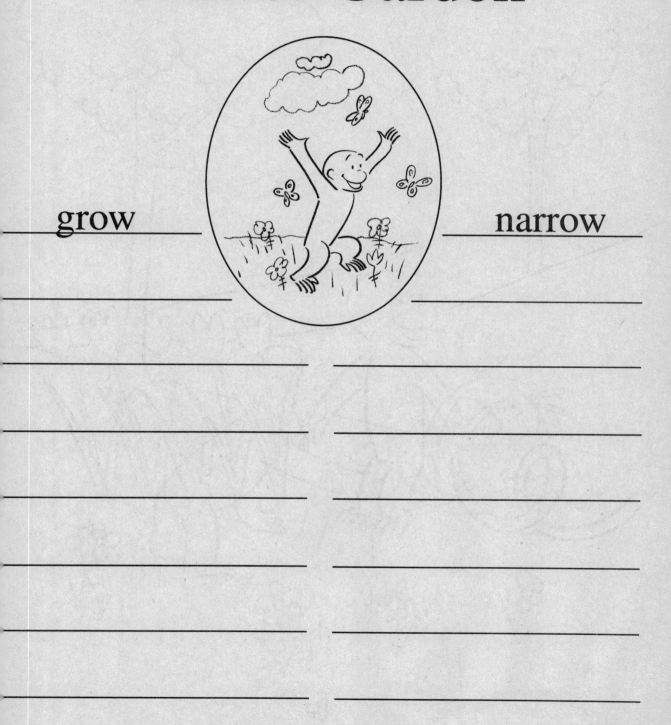

grow

narrow

You Can Draw!

Use the grid to draw Curious George.

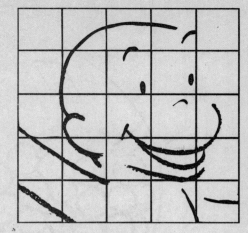

George loves gumballs!

Dalmatian Press

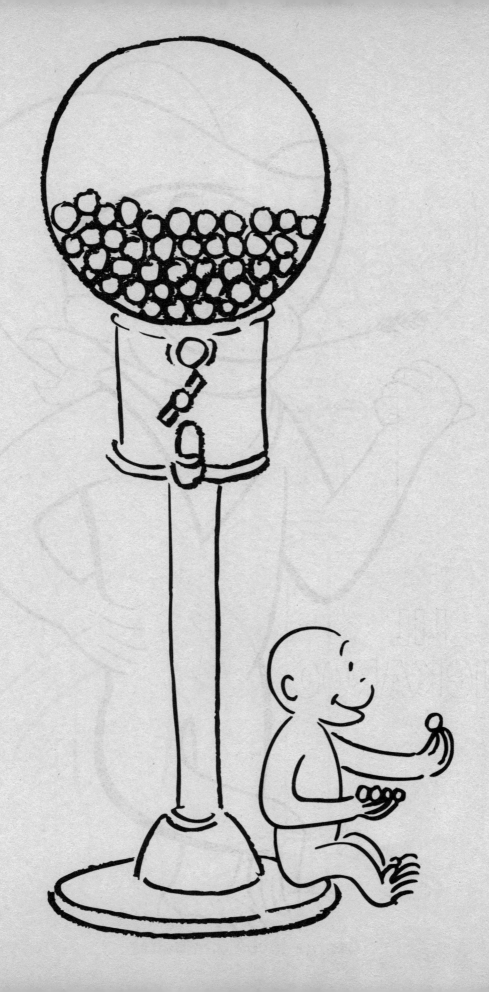

LIL'
BUCKAROO

Help George find his treasure chest.

Start

Finish

Guess Who?

Circle your answer.

Playing in the rain!

Finish the Picture

Be an artist!
Draw Curious George's
fish.

Secret Message

Lift the bottom of the page toward you and
view from the bottom.

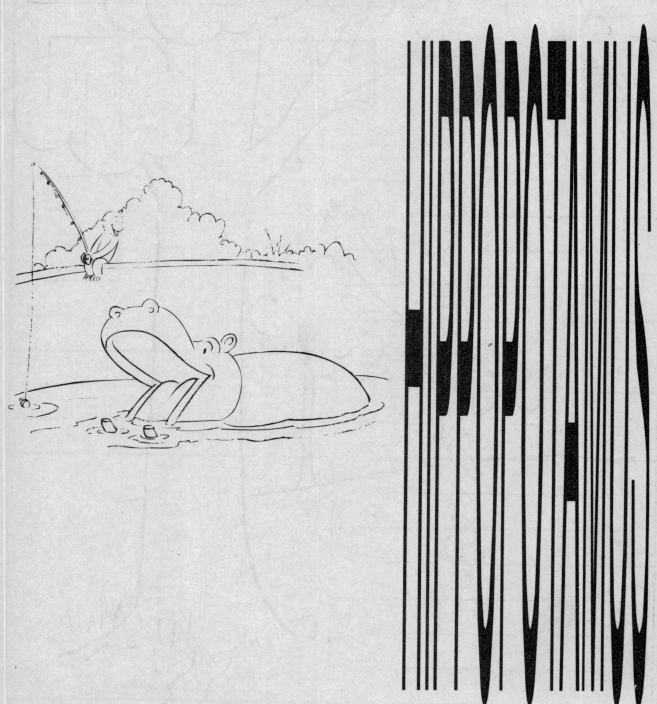

Dalmatian Press

Secret Message

Lift the bottom of the page toward you and view from the bottom.

Answer: Sandwich

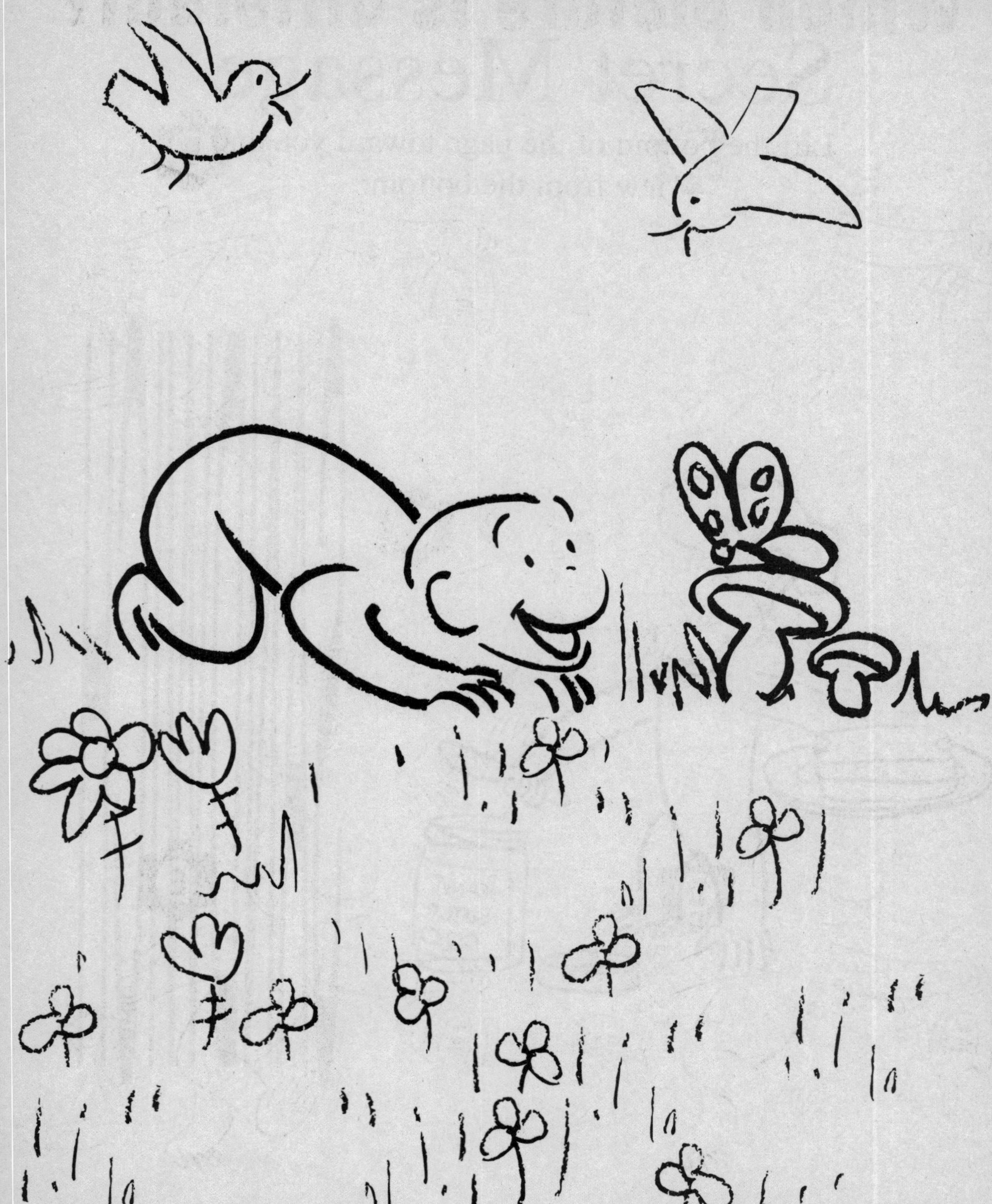

Which picture is different?

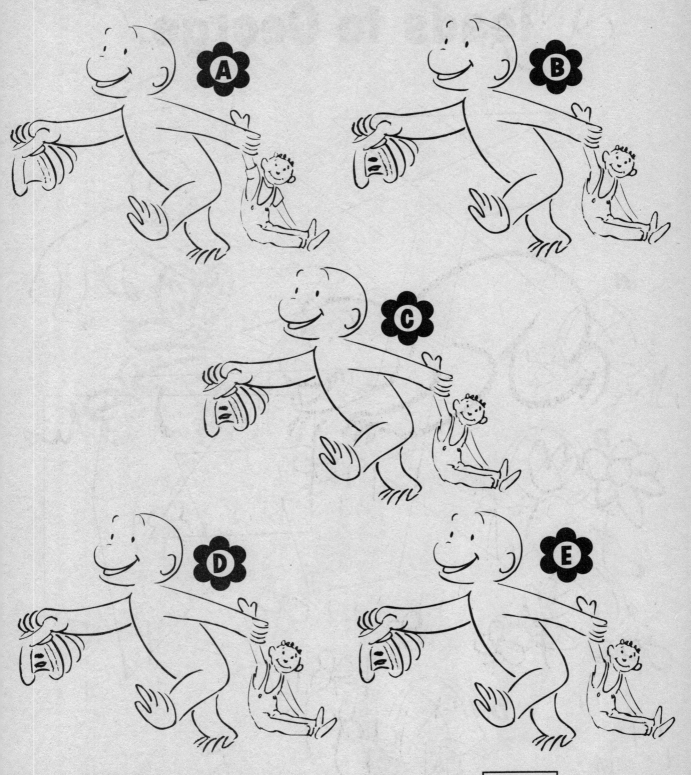

Your answer:

Circle the turtle that leads to George.

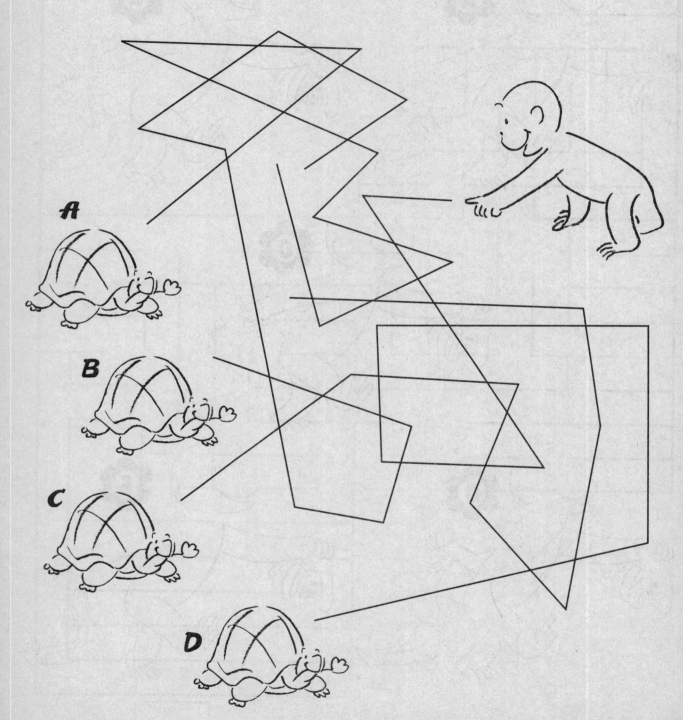

Help George get to his balloon.

Finish

Start

Connect the DOTS

Dalmatian Press

You Can Draw!

Use the grid to draw
George in his chef's hat.

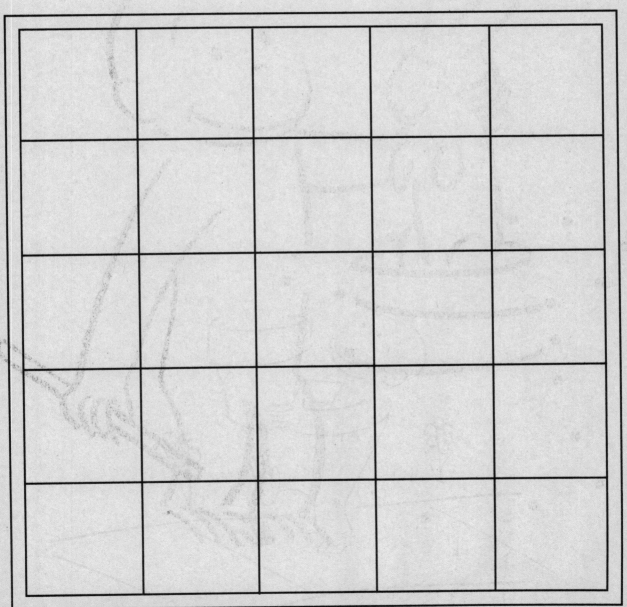

Finish the Picture

Be an artist!
Draw all the flowers
in George's pot.

Secret Message

Lift the bottom of the page toward you and view from the bottom.

Dalmatian Press

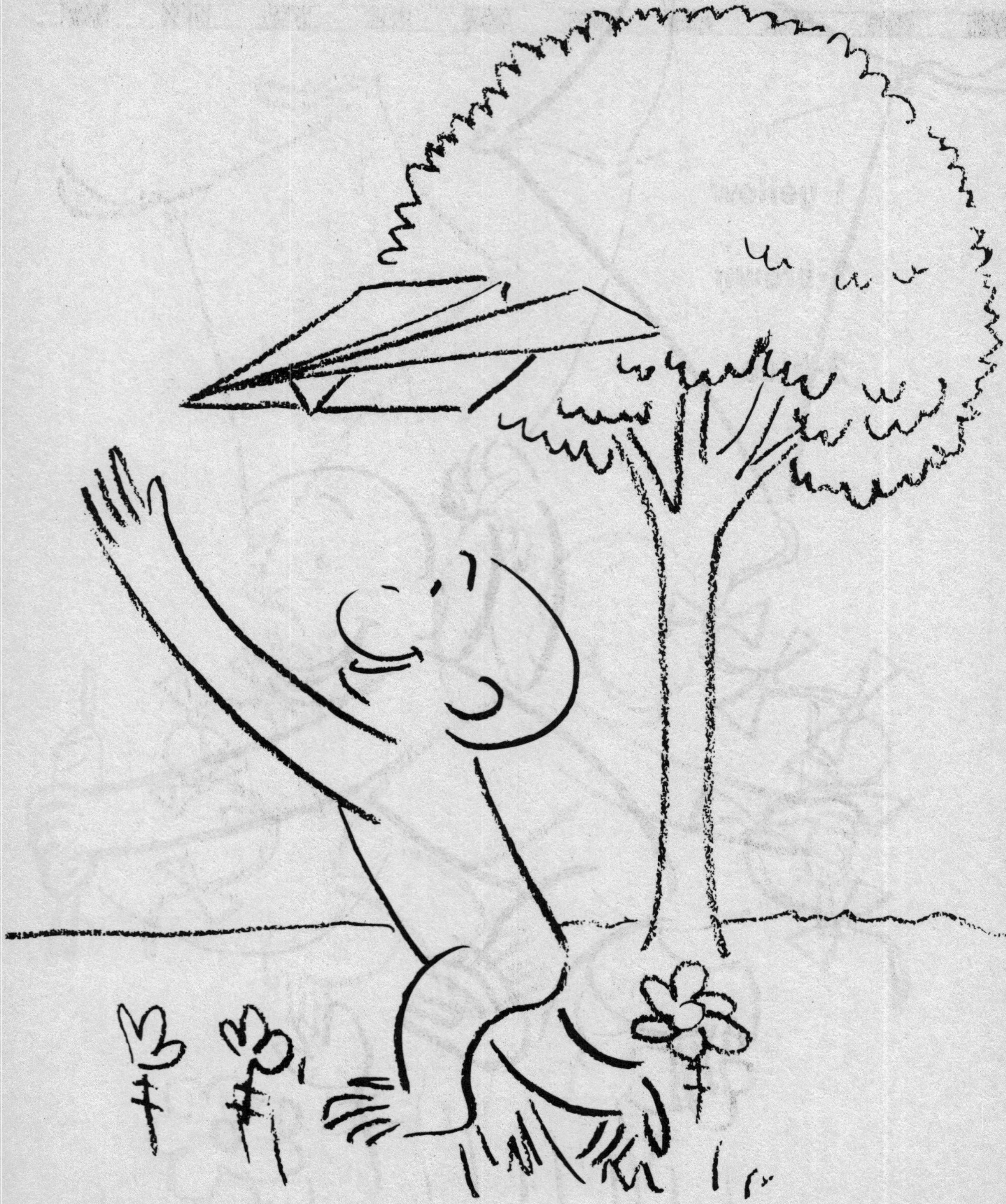

Color By Number

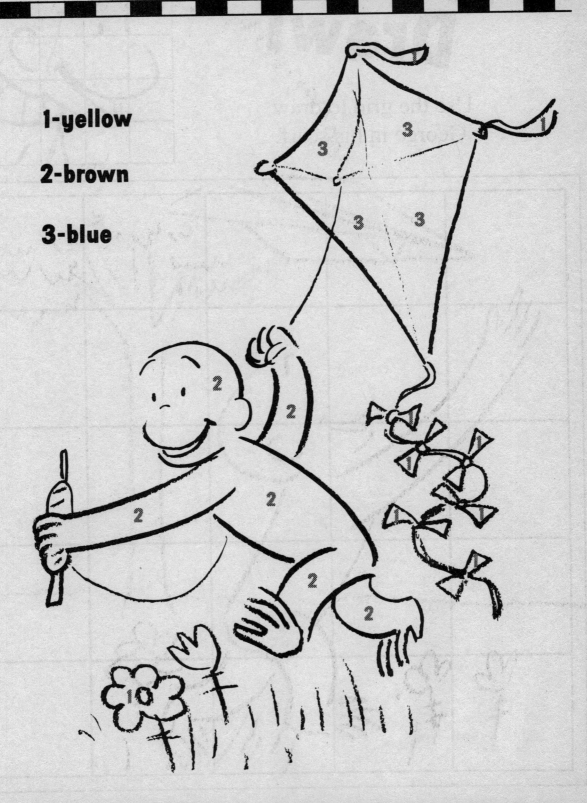

1-yellow

2-brown

3-blue

You Can Draw!

Use the grid to draw George in his scarf.

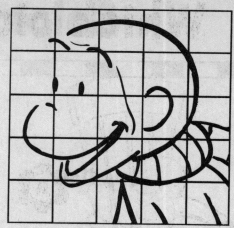

Which picture is different?

333

Your answer:

Guess Who?

Circle your answer.

Fireman George

Pirate George

Chef George

Painter George

Dalmatian Press

George at the seashore.

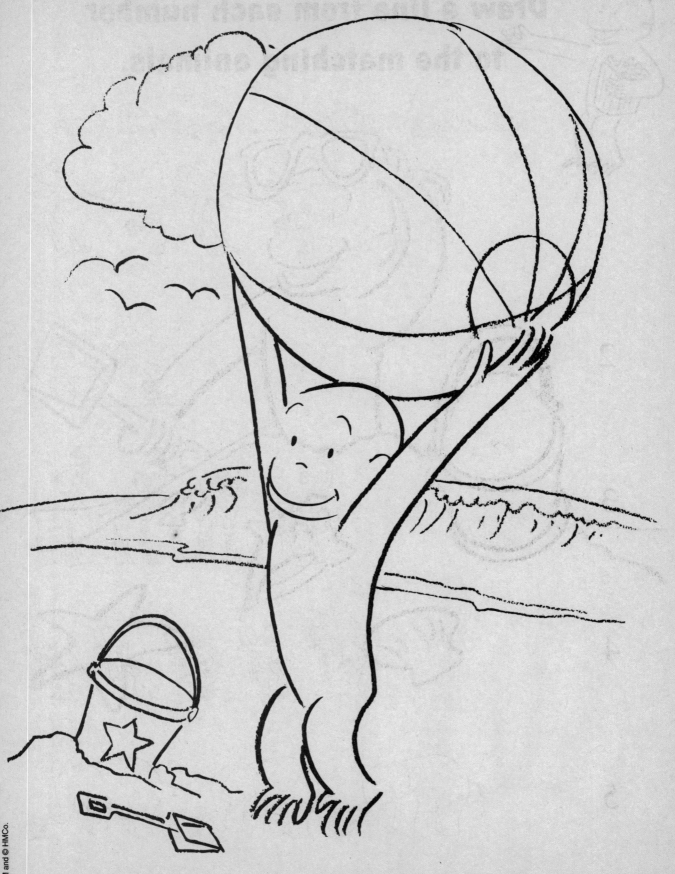

Draw a line from each number to the matching animals.

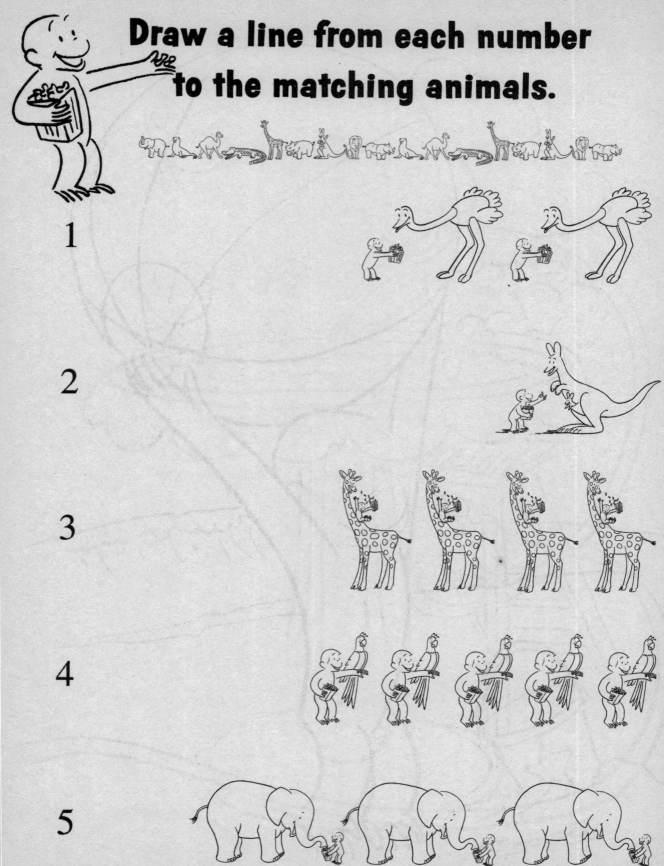

1

2

3

4

5

Secret Message

Lift the bottom of the page toward you and
view from the bottom.

Dalmatian Press

Circle the line that leads George to the fish.

Answer: C

Guess Who?

Circle your answer.

Curious George

Froggie

Hippo

Camel

Dalmatian Press

Yards and yards of spaghetti!

How many words can you make from the letters in:

Stepladder

pal

tea

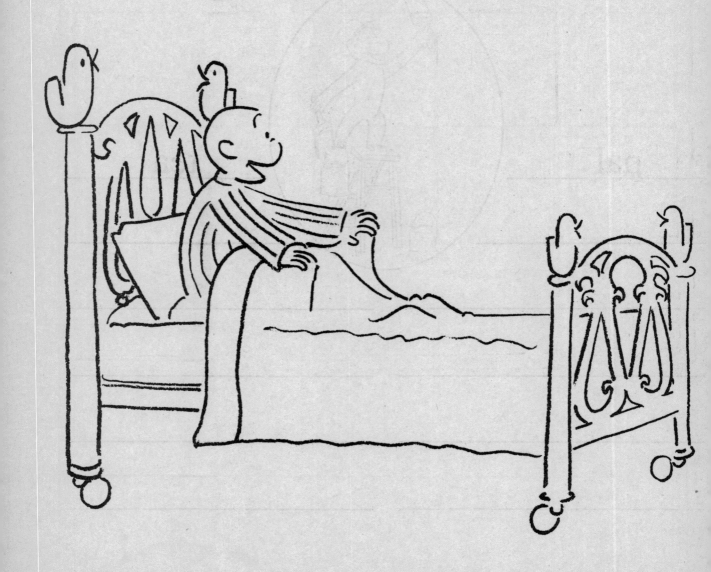

**"Rise and shine, George.
Let's make pancakes!"**

George is very hungry.

Draw a line from each item to its shadow.

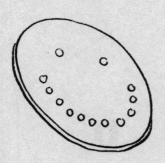

Which stack is different?

A

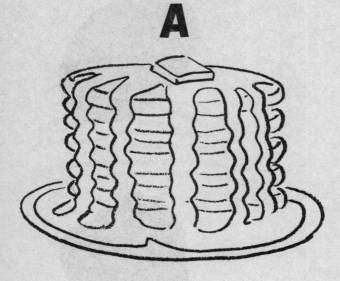

B

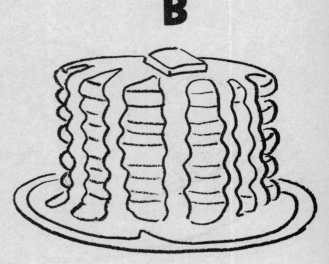

C

D

Your answer:

What goes with pancakes?

A pat of butter...

....and maple syrup!

And blueberries! Let's eat!

How many donuts do you count?

Your answer:

George loves to eat fruit.

Dalmatian Press

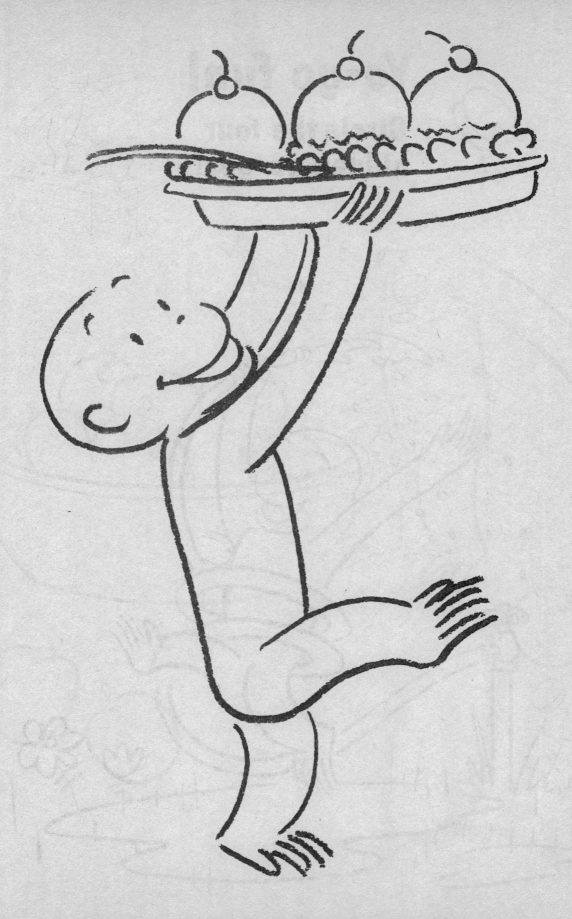

Ice-cream sundaes are yummy, too!

Yo-yo fun!

Circle the four hidden yo-yos!

George likes donuts and books!

Color By Number

1-yellow   **2-brown**   **3-red**

Curious Crossword!

Fill in the blanks to finish the puzzle.

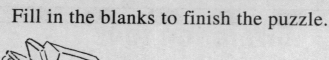

Across

1. George likes to eat ——————— for breakfast.

Down

2. What goes with pancakes? Maple ———————.

3. Don't forget a pat of ———————.

Sweet Surprise

Circle the four
hidden pieces of cake!

Match the monkeys to the correct numbers.

1   

2   

3   

4   

5   

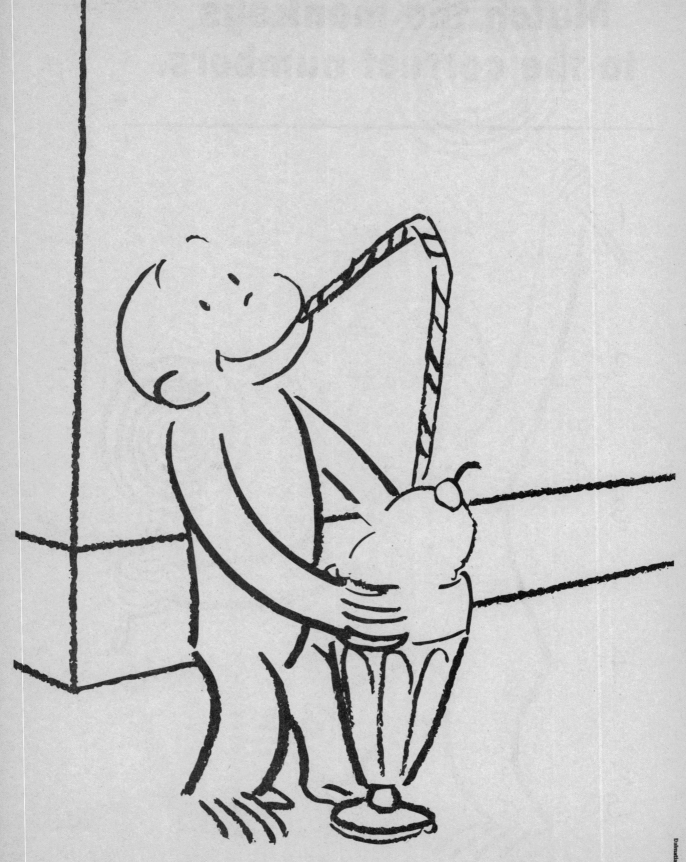

Lots of lollipops!

An extra-big bag of donuts!

How many alligators do you count?

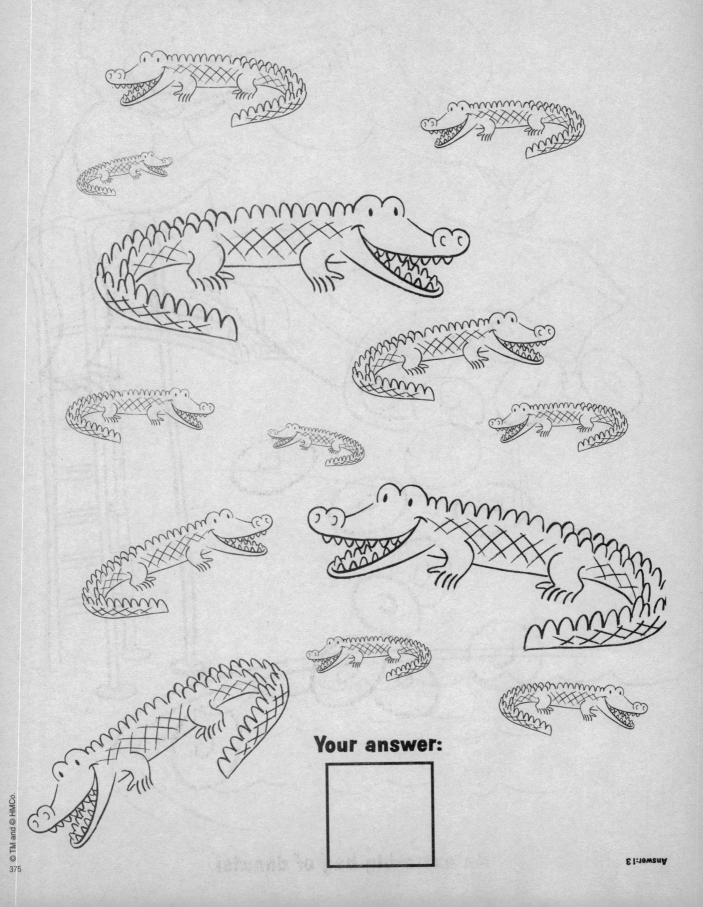

Your answer:

375

Color By Number

1-green   **2-brown**   **3-blue**

Match the animal to its shadow.

Write the correct letter in the box next to the picture.

Dalmatian Press

Circle the picture of George that does not belong.

Answer: George on a unicycle

Circle the picture of George that does not belong.

How many lollipops do you count?

Your answer:

Dalmatian Press

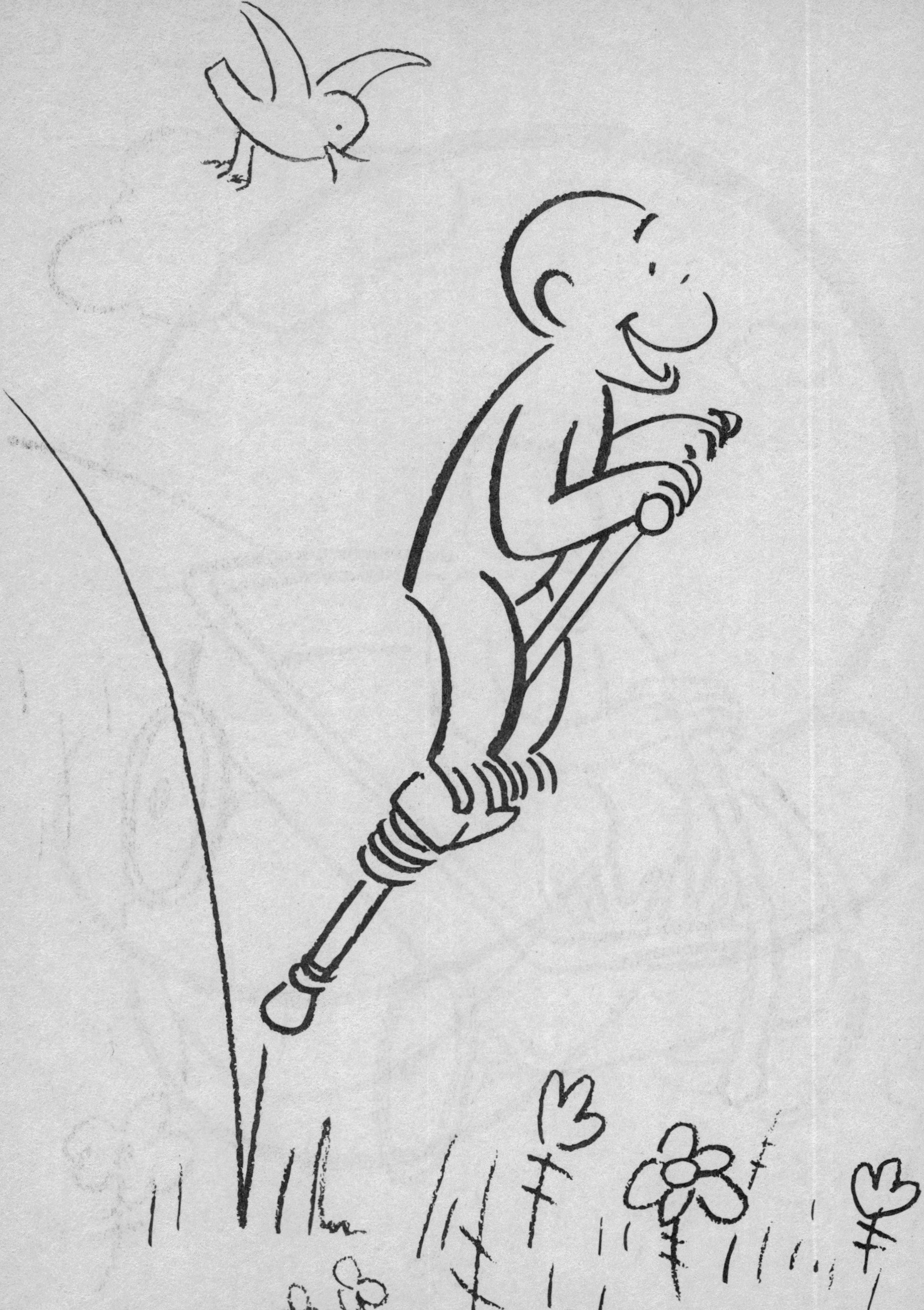

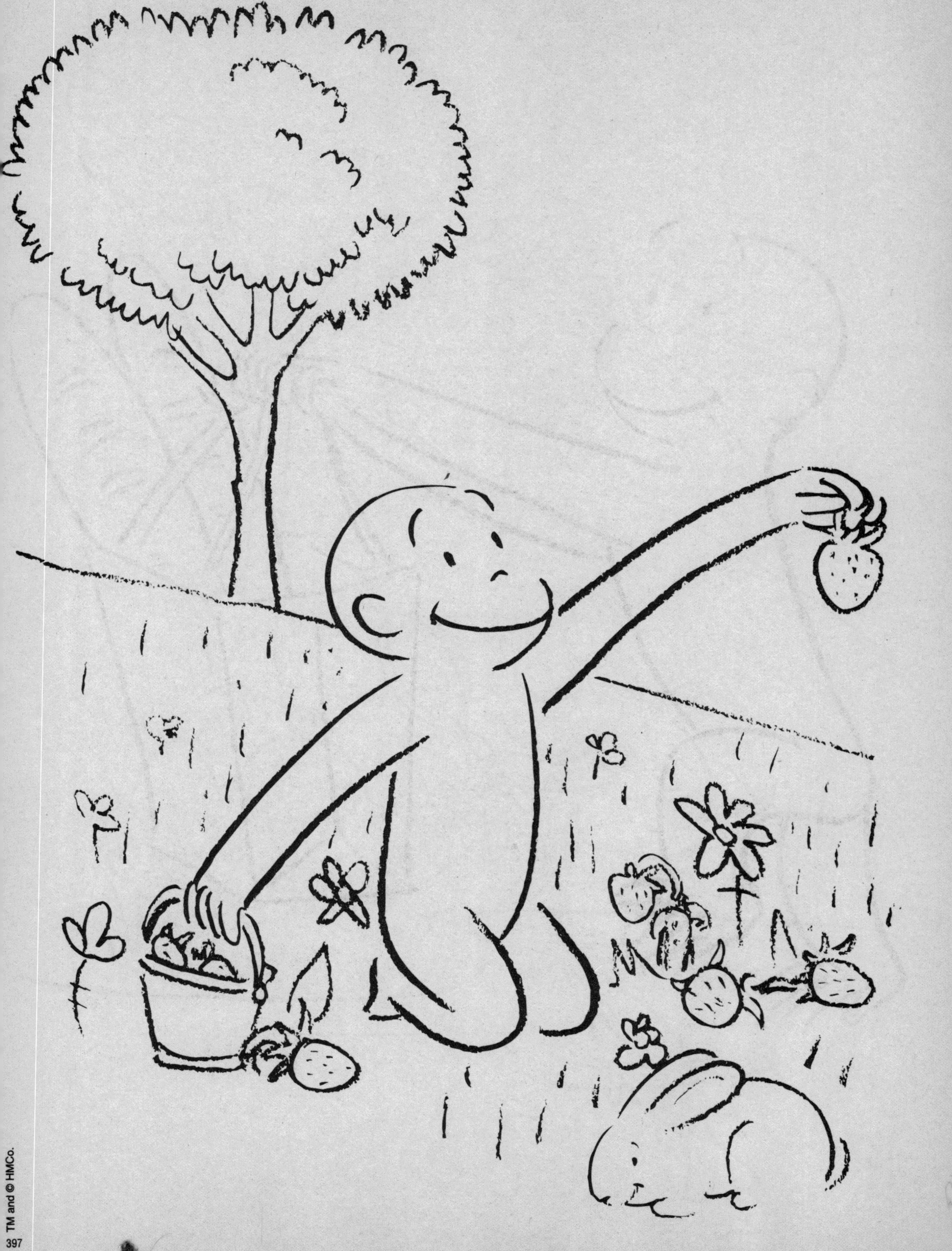

Hanging
Around